Tuck Me In

18 CUTE & CUDDLY QUILTS FOR KIDS

From the Editors and Contributors of *Quiltmaker* Magazine

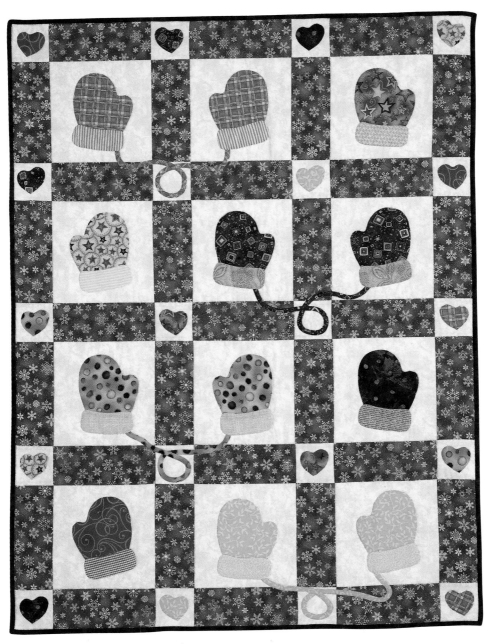

C&T PUBLISHING

Text and artwork © 2005 Primedia Enthusiast Group

Publisher: Amy Marson

Editorial Director: Gailen Runge

Acquisitions Editor: Jan Grigsby

Editor: Lynn Koolish

Technical Editors: Elin Thomas and Wendy Mathson

Copyeditor/Proofreader: Wordfirm, Inc.

Cover Designer: Kristen Yenche

Book Designer: Susan H. Hartman

Production Assistant: Kerry Graham

Photography: Mellisa Mahoney Karlin

Published by C&T Publishing, Inc., P.O. Box 1456, Lafayette, CA 94549

Library of Congress Cataloging-in-Publication Data

Tuck me in : 18 cute & cuddly quilts for kids / from the editors and contributors of Quiltmaker magazine.

p. cm.

Includes bibliographical references.

ISBN 1-57120-315-X (paper trade)

1. Patchwork—Patterns. 2. Quilting. 3. Children's quilts. 4. Crib quilts. I. Quiltmaker. II. Title.

TT835.T77 2005

746.46'041—dc22

2005007325

Printed in Singapore

10 9 8 7 6 5 4 3 2 1

Contents

Preface

Creating quilts for children is a time-honored tradition, whether for your own children, for nieces, nephews, or grandchildren, or for friends.

Making charity or comfort quilts is also a tradition among quilters. There are many ways to contribute—giving fabric or time, joining in for a day of tying quilts, making quilt tops, or making the entire quilt. A great way to improve your machine quilting skills, especially free-motion machine quilting, is to practice on a kid-sized quilt that will be given to someone who will love it, no matter what the quilting looks like.

Your local quilt guild is a good place to start if you'd like to be involved in making quilts for kids on either a regular or an occasional basis. There are nationwide organizations with local chapters (we've listed a few of the many organizations in the Resources, page 80). You can also contact a local social service agency to find out about hospitals, hospices, shelters, or other organizations where you might volunteer or make a donation.

So, when you make a kid's quilt, think about making two. It doesn't take much longer—one for you to give to a child you know and one to give to a child you don't know, but who will appreciate it more than you can ever imagine.

Project Linus Day 2005 at Quiltmaker magazine. In February 2005, 100 volunteers came to the Quiltmaker offices in Golden, Colorado, to make quilts for Project Linus.

Stars and Moon

**Designed and made by
Nancy Taylor.
Fabrics from P&B Textiles.
Modeled by
Forrest Gauch.**

When Nancy Taylor of Pleasanton, California, and her husband celebrated the arrival of their first grandchild, she expressed her happiness by creating three baby quilts for the little one. *Stars and Moon* is one of those quilts—a simple pattern designed for a wonderful array of flannels.

Materials and Cutting

QUILT SIZES:	Crib/Wall Quilt (shown)	Twin Comforter
	44″ × 44″	72″ × 93″
FINISHED BLOCK SIZE:		
7″ × 7″		
YARDAGE		
Multiprint Scraps	1¼ yards	3½ yards
	13 A	54 A
Tone-on-Tone Scraps	1¼ yards	3⅔ yards
	92 B	304 B
Yellow Solid	1¼ yards	2½ yards
border 1 sides*	2 at 1½″ × 35½″	2 at 1½″ × 84½″
border 1 top/bottom*	2 at 1½″ × 37½″	2 at 1½″ × 65½″
	12 stars, 1 moon	49 stars, 5 moons
Green Print	scrap	scrap
	8 C	8 C
Blue Print	⅝ yard	⅞ yard
double-fold binding	6 at 2¼″ × 34″	10 at 2¼″ × 37″
Backing	2⅞ yards	5¾ yards
panels	2 at 25″ × 48″	2 at 39″ × 97″
sleeve	1 at 9″ × 44″	none for this size
Batting	48″ x 48″	76″ x 97″

SUPPLIES: paper-backed fusible web, stabilizer (optional), embroidery floss

*Seam allowance is included in the length, but no extra has been added for insurance.

Getting Started

For more detailed directions on quiltmaking, see Quilting Basics (pages 76–79).

Directions are for both the crib/wall quilt and the twin comforter. Information specific to the twin size is given in brackets [ ].

Easy piecing and fused appliqué make this a quick project. To simplify the pattern instructions, the yardage information lists all the appliqué from one yellow solid fabric, but you may want to mix colors, as Nancy did. The appliqué patches are presented in reverse for the fusing technique; patches are fused, and then the edges are secured with a blanket stitch. For help doing this by machine, see Machine Blanket Stitch (page 8). If you prefer to sew by hand, you won't need to use a stabilizer. See the blanket stitch illustration on page 8.

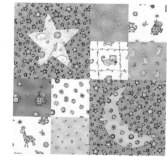

In this pastel version, notice the light B patches create a strong diagonal line.

Making the Blocks

1 Trace the required number of stars and moon[s] on the paper side of the fusible web. Following the manufacturer's directions, iron the fusible web to the wrong side of the fabric. Cut out the patches on the drawn lines. Remove the paper backing. Position each star and moon on an A patch, and iron in place. By hand or machine, blanket stitch around the edges of each fused patch.

Star Block
Make 12 [49]

Moon Block
Make 1 [5]

2 By eye, mark the mouth and eye on the moon[s] and then satin stitch them by machine or by hand. Tear away any stabilizer. Center each motif, and trim the A patches to 7½″ × 7½″.

3 Arrange colors as you like, and join the B's to make the Four-Patches. Press the seam allowances as shown.

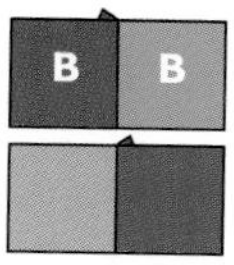

Four-Patch Piecing
Make 12 [54]

Completing the Center

1 Make 5 [12] rows of alternating Four-Patches and appliqué blocks as shown in the Quilt Assembly diagram. Press the seam allowances toward the appliqué blocks.

2 Join the rows and press all seam allowances in the same direction.

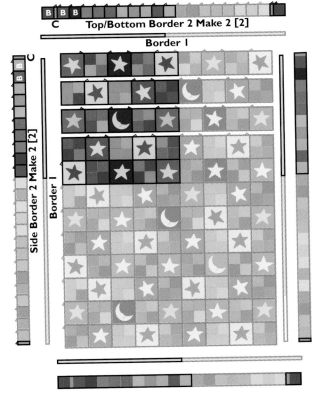

Quilt Assembly
Crib/wall quilt is shown in darker colors.
Twin comforter includes the complete diagram.

Adding the Borders

1 To piece a side strip for border 2, join 10 [24] B's and then sew a C to each end. Make 2 [2]. For each border 2 top and bottom strip, join 10 [18] B patches. To the ends of these strips, add a C and another B.

2 Sew the border 1 side strips to the quilt, matching centers and ends, easing if necessary. Press the seam allowances toward the strips. In the same way, add the border 1 top and bottom strips.

3 Sew the border 2 side strips to the quilt, matching centers and ends. Press the seam allowances toward the quilt center. Repeat to add the border 2 top and bottom strips.

Quilting and Finishing

1 Refer to the Quilting Placement diagram to mark the *You're a Star!* quilting motif in the border 2 corners, the Four-Patches, and the Moon blocks. Instead of marking, you can trace the motif on contact paper and cut it out to make a repositionable template. Stick the template on your sandwiched quilt, quilt around the shape, and then move the template to another area for more quilting. Remove this sticky paper after each quilting session.

Quilting Placement

2 Layer the backing, batting, and quilt top. Baste the layers together.

3 Quilt in-the-ditch the blocks, appliqué, and border 1. Following the patchwork, quilt diagonal lines through the Four-Patches as shown. Quilt as marked, adding squiggly quilting around the appliqués and in border 2.

4 Sew the binding strips end to end to make a continuous binding. Bind the edges of the quilt.

5 To display the wall quilt, sew a sleeve to the backing.

You're a Star!
Quilting

Machine Blanket Stitch

Machine blanket stitch can be a quick and easy way to appliqué if you keep the following tips in mind:

- Stabilize your work under each background patch to prevent puckering and to support the heavy stitching. Look for stabilizers, such as Sulky's Tear-Easy or Solvy, at your favorite quilt shop. As an alternative, use typing paper pinned to the wrong side of the background, or try freezer paper ironed to the wrong side.

- To replicate this quilt's appliqué, set the length of your blanket stitch to 8–10 stitches per inch (2.5–3.5 metric) and about the same for the width. Feel free to experiment with other settings to create a different look.

- The straight stitch should lie as close to the patch edge as possible, with the zigzag piercing the appliqué.

- Refer to the illustration for instructions on sewing the points. As you blanket stitch a point or a curve, pivot with the needle down on a straight stitch rather than on a zigzag.

- When approaching points on appliqué patches, shorten or lengthen the straight stitch as necessary to ensure that a zigzag will pierce point ends to secure the patch.

- Practice machine blanket stitching on a sample to determine your stitch length and width and to practice negotiating curves and points.

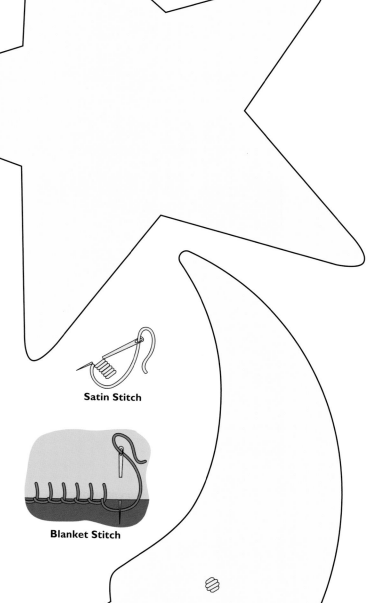

Satin Stitch

Blanket Stitch

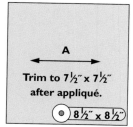

A

Trim to 7½″ x 7½″ after appliqué.

8½″ x 8½″

Align arrows with lengthwise or crosswise grain of fabric.

B

4″ x 4″

C

1½″ x 4″

Motifs are reversed for fusible appliqué.

Sleep Over

This quilt is a perfect way to share your love of quilts with a special child in your life! Make a wall quilt that shows six little quilts on six little beds, and then add the dolls, ready for their slumber party. An easy construction method eliminates tiny patches for hands and feet.

**Designed and made by
Caroline Reardon.
Modeled by
Sophie Reardon Capp.**

QUILT SIZE:	Wall Quilt/Dolls
	26¼" × 21¾"

FINISHED BLOCK SIZES:
5¼" × 7¼", 4½" × 4½"

YARDAGE

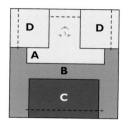

For Each Doll	scraps
skin-tone solid	1 A, 4 D
hair-color solid	1 A
nightgown print	2 B
slippers print	2 C
For Each Quilt	scraps
assorted prints	E, F as shown in block diagrams
pastel solid	1 I
flannel	1 I
For Each Bed	scraps
light print	1 G, 1 H
medium-light print	1 I
medium print	1 K
medium-dark print	1 L
Gold Print	⅝ yard
top/bottom border*	2 at 3½" × 26¾"
sash*	1 at 1¾" × 26¾"
	12 J, 4 M, 4 N
Gold and White Stripe	⅜ yard
double-fold binding	3 at 2¼" × 40"
Backing	1 yard
panel	1 at 26" × 31"
sleeve	1 at 9" × 26"
Batting	26" × 31"

SUPPLIES: polyester fiberfill; red and black fine-line, permanent-ink fabric pens; pink crayon; yarn for hair; 3" × 4½" cardboard; narrow ribbon for hair ties

*Seam allowance is included in the length, but no extra has been added for insurance.

Getting Started

For more detailed directions on quiltmaking, see Quilting Basics (pages 76–79).

When you're done, hang the quilt within easy reach of little hands. This charming wall quilt will keep the six little dolls safe and warm until their next playtime.

Making the Dolls

The construction of this doll is quite easy. You'll just sew rectangles into units, stitch the figure shape onto these units, and then cut out around the figure.

1 First position the A patch of skin-tone fabric right side up over the A patch pattern. With a light source underneath, use permanent-ink pens to trace the face. For more friendly faces, see below.

2 To make a front unit, center patch A wrong side out with the face upside down on the edge of B. Join with a ¼" seam. Join C to the bottom of B in the same way. Align D's with the top corners of B and join as shown.

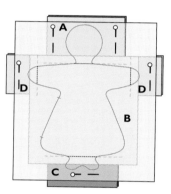

3 Press the patches open with all seam allowances away from B. Repeat for the back unit using the hair-color A patch. With right sides together, pin the units together, matching seams.

4 Transfer the doll outline to tracing paper. Pin the paper to the layered units, positioning the dotted lines on the seams as shown. Sew on the outline using a very short stitch (15–20 per inch or 2–1.5 metric) and backstitching at both sides of the opening. Tear away the paper.

5 At the opening, trim seam allowances to ¼". Trim remaining seam to ⅛". Clip close to the stitching at all inside curves, and notch all outside curves.

6 Turn right side out. Stuff the hands and arms with fiberfill. By hand or machine, stitch through all thicknesses from shoulder to underarm on each side (see dashed lines on pattern); this will allow the arms to bend. Complete the stuffing. Turn in the seam allowances along the opening and ladder stitch to close.

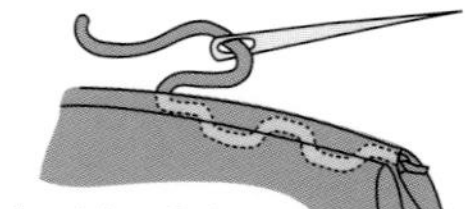

Ladder Stitch

7 To make the hair, cut a piece of cardboard 3″ × 4½″. Wrap the yarn lengthwise 8–12 complete times (finer yarn requires more wraps). Slide the yarn off the cardboard. Use short stitches to machine stitch across and back at the center, keeping the width of the wrapped yarn at 1½″.

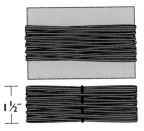

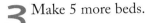

8 Position the stitching as the center part, and hand sew to the head. Clip yarn loops at the ends, and arrange strands for the hairdo you like, trimming and then tacking the yarn in place. Add ribbons as desired.

9 Use a pink crayon to make rosy cheeks.

Making the Bed Quilts

1 Use scraps of your choice and follow the block diagrams to make the 6 quilt tops shown.

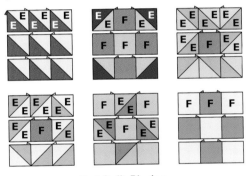

Bed Quilt Piecing

2 For each quilt, layer in order: the flannel I patch, the pastel I patch (backing) right side up, and the quilt top wrong side up. Stitch the layers together using a ¼″ seam allowance. Leave a 1½″ opening along one side. Turn right side out, stitch the opening closed, and press. Quilt all the patches in-the-ditch.

Making the Beds

1 To make the pillow, fold H in half lengthwise, right sides together. On each side, stitch a line ¼″ long and ¼″ from the fold; backstitch. Open H, and pin right side up on top of G. Sew ³⁄₁₆″ from the raw edges around 3 sides. Stuff lightly with fiberfill and sew the remaining side closed.

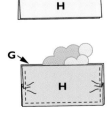

2 Join the pillow (G/H) to I in a ¼″ seam. Sew the J background pieces to the K and L patches as indicated. Then complete the block, setting in J/L after K/J has been sewn to H/I.

3 Make 5 more beds.

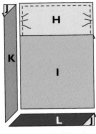

**Bed Block Piecing
Make 6**

Completing the Top

1 Follow the Quilt Assembly diagram, and join the beds, M's, and N's to make the rows. Press the seam allowances away from the beds.

2 Sew the sash between the rows, matching centers and ends. Add the top and bottom border strips. Press these seam allowances toward the sash and border strips.

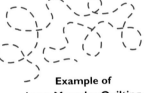

Quilt Assembly

Quilting and Finishing

1 For the *Loop Meander* quilting by machine (shown in the photographed quilt), layer and baste the backing, batting, and quilt top now.

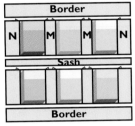

**Example of
Loop Meander Quilting**

OR

For the *Dancing Dolls* quilting, trace the motif. Following the Quilting Placement diagram, mark a doll in each corner and several dolls along the M patches. Mark the perimeter, matching dots to repeat. Then layer and baste.

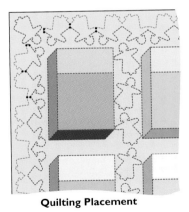

Quilting Placement

2 Quilt in-the-ditch the H/I seams and beds. Quilt the remaining areas in whichever pattern you have chosen. If you machine quilt the marked motifs, quilt the red and the blue lines in the diagram as separate paths.

3 On each bed quilt, turn down and tack the upper right corner. Appliqué 3 sides of each bed quilt onto I, angling in the edges to form a pocket for the doll. Reinforce both sides of the opening with extra stitches.

4 Sew the binding strips end to end to make a continuous binding. Bind the edges of the quilt.

5 Add a sleeve, and then hang the quilt conveniently so the dolls can be taken to their slumber party once playtime is over.

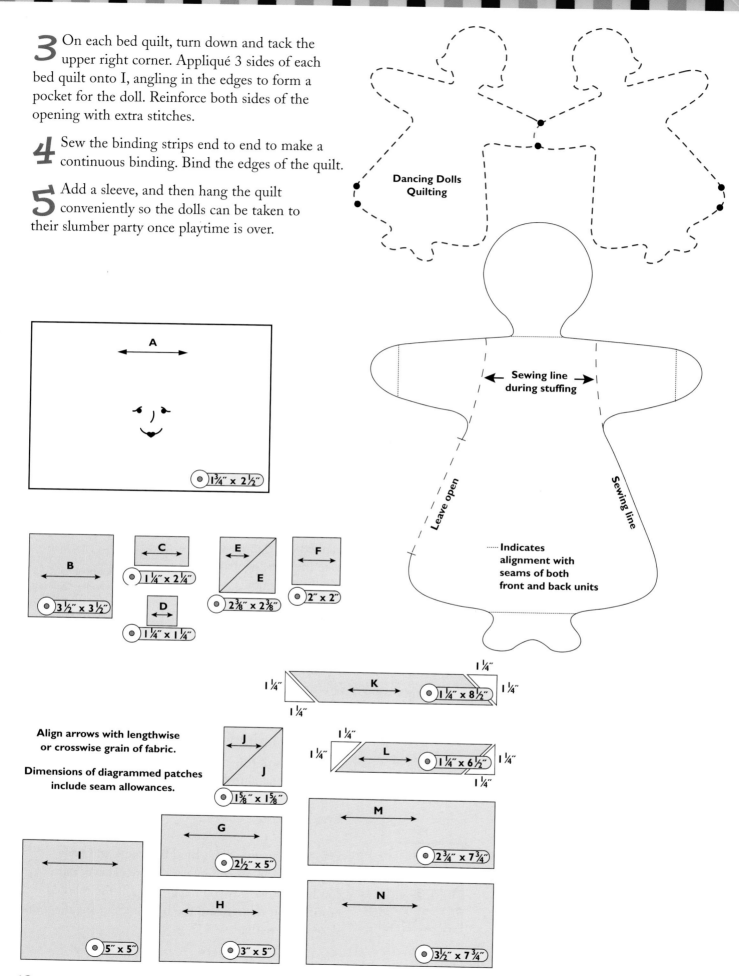

Dancing Dolls Quilting

A

$1\frac{3}{4}'' \times 2\frac{1}{2}''$

B
$3\frac{1}{2}'' \times 3\frac{1}{2}''$

C
$1\frac{1}{4}'' \times 2\frac{1}{4}''$

D
$1\frac{1}{4}'' \times 1\frac{1}{4}''$

E
E
$2\frac{3}{8}'' \times 2\frac{3}{8}''$

F
$2'' \times 2''$

Sewing line during stuffing

Leave open

Sewing line

······ Indicates alignment with seams of both front and back units

$1\frac{1}{4}''$

K
$1\frac{1}{4}''$ $1\frac{1}{4}'' \times 8\frac{1}{2}''$ $1\frac{1}{4}''$

$1\frac{1}{4}''$

Align arrows with lengthwise or crosswise grain of fabric.

Dimensions of diagrammed patches include seam allowances.

J
J
$1\frac{5}{8}'' \times 1\frac{5}{8}''$

$1\frac{1}{4}''$

L
$1\frac{1}{4}''$ $1\frac{1}{4}'' \times 6\frac{1}{2}''$ $1\frac{1}{4}''$

$1\frac{1}{4}''$

M
$2\frac{3}{4}'' \times 7\frac{3}{4}''$

G
$2\frac{1}{2}'' \times 5''$

I

N
$3\frac{1}{2}'' \times 7\frac{3}{4}''$

H
$3'' \times 5''$

$5'' \times 5''$

Bear Claws

Designed by
Sandra Gould,
made by Mickie Swall.
Fabrics from P&B Textiles
and Chanteclaire Fabrics.
Modeled by
Kathleen Eisinger.

S andra Gould of Sussex, New Jersey, adapted the traditional Maple Leaf block and arranged the lights and darks to create movement in this quilt that will delight any child or teen.

FINISHED BLOCK SIZE:
15″ × 15″

QUILT SIZES:	Long Double Comforter (shown) 82½″ × 97½″	Queen Comforter 97½″ × 97½″
YARDAGE		
Dark Purple Dots	2½ yards	2⅝ yards
border 4 sides*	2 at 5½″ × 85″	2 at 5½″ × 85″
border 4 top/bottom*	2 at 5½″ × 70″	2 at 5½″ × 85″
	44 A, 40 B	54 A, 50 B
Light Purple Print	1½ yards	1⅝ yards
double-fold binding	10 at 2¼″ × 40″	11 at 2¼″ × 40″
folded border strips	8 at 1½″ × 40″	9 at 1½″ × 40″
	40 A	50 A
Red Print	2½ yards	2⅝ yards
border 2 sides*	2 at 1¾″ × 82½″	2 at 1¾″ × 82½″
border 2 top/bottom*	2 at 1¾″ × 70″	2 at 1¾″ × 85″
	44 A, 176 C	54 A, 216 C
Orange Dots	1 yard	1⅛ yards
	160 C	200 C
Orange Grid	1 yard	1⅛ yards
	176 C	216 C
Medium Green Print	⅜ yard	½ yard
	40 A	50 A
Lime Green Print	1⅓ yards	1½ yards
	40 A, 160 C	50 A, 200 C
Green Dots	2½ yards	2½ yards
border 3 sides*	2 at 3″ × 85″	2 at 3″ × 85″
border 3 top/bottom*	2 at 3″ × 70″	2 at 3″ × 85″
	40 A, 40 B	50 A, 50 B
Gold Print	2¼ yards	2½ yards
border 1 sides*	2 at 3″ × 77½″	2 at 3″ × 77½″
border 1 top/bottom*	2 at 3″ × 67½″	2 at 3″ × 82½″
	4 A, 4 B	4 A, 4 B
Backing	7¾ yards	9⅛ yards
panels	3 at 35″ × 87″	3 at 35″ × 102″
Batting	87″ × 102″	102″ × 102″

*An extra 2″ have been added to the length for insurance.

If you use the method described in the Triangle Squares tip, do not cut the patches listed in colored type.

Triangle Squares

Instead of joining individually cut C patches, use this assembly method to avoid working with stretchy bias edges.

First cut the border strips from the red print; then cut 99 [109] squares 3⅜″ × 3⅜″ from both the red print and the orange grid fabrics. With right sides together and the lighter fabric on top, pair a red print and an orange grid square. Draw a diagonal line from corner to corner, and stitch ¼″ out on both sides of the line. Cut along the line. Open the C's,

and press the seams toward the darker patches. Make 176 [216] triangle squares from these two fabrics.

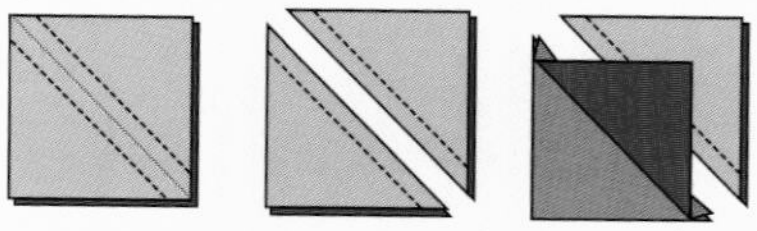

Use this method to join 80 [100] squares 3⅜″ × 3⅜″ each of lime green and orange dot fabrics to make 160 [200] triangle squares needed for the blocks.

Getting Started

For more detailed directions on quiltmaking, see Quilting Basics (pages 76–79).

Directions are for both the long double and queen comforters. Information specific to the queen size is given in brackets [ ].

This quilt includes a folded border, which enhances the design and adds dimension to the quilt. If you prefer, you can omit this feature without affecting any border measurements.

Making the Center

1 Refer to the diagrams to make the blocks and corner units. Press the seam allowances as shown.

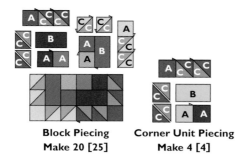

Block Piecing
Make 20 [25]

Corner Unit Piecing
Make 4 [4]

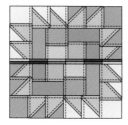

Block Pressing

2 Orient all the blocks in the same direction, and sew the blocks together to make each row. Press the seam allowances of every other row in the same direction.

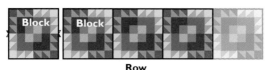

Row
Make 5 [5]
Long double comforter is shown in darker colors.
Queen comforter includes the complete diagram.

3 Join the rows, and then press the seam allowances in the same direction.

Adding Borders 1 and 2

1 Sew the border 1 side strips to the quilt. Press the seam allowances toward the strips, and trim any extra length. In the same way, add the border 1 top and bottom strips.

2 To make the folded border, join 8 [9] light purple print strips to make 1 long strip. With wrong sides together, fold the strip in half along the length, and press. Cut this strip into 2 strips 82½″ [82½″] long for the side and 2 strips 70″ [85″] long for the top and bottom.

3 Baste each folded border strip to the corresponding border 1 strip and trim any extra length.

4 Add the border 2 side strips, pressing the seam allowances away from the quilt's center and keeping the folded border strips against the border 1 strips. Trim any extra length.

5 Repeat for the top and bottom border 2 strips.

Adding Borders 3 and 4

1 Join the corresponding border 3 and border 4 strips to make 4 border units. Press the seam allowances toward the border 4 strips.

2 After pressing the quilt top, measure the quilt from raw edge to raw edge through the vertical center. Trim the side border units to this measurement. In the same way, measure the horizontal center and trim the top and bottom border units to this measurement. Orient the corner units as shown in the photograph and sew a unit to each end of the top and bottom border units. Press the seam allowances toward the border units.

3 Match centers and ends. Add the side border units first and then add the top and bottom. Press the seam allowances away from the quilt's center.

Quilting and Finishing

1 Mark the *Cinnamon Swirl* quilting in the blocks as shown. Mark 8 [10] border motifs in the border 4 top and bottom strips and mark 10 [10] motifs in the border 4 side strips, adjusting the motifs as needed.

Quilting Placement

2 Layer the backing, batting, and quilt top. Baste the layers together.

3 Stitch the outline quilting ⅜″ from the seamlines. Outline quilt the C patches and borders 1 and 3. Quilt the marked motifs and quilt a line in the center of border 2.

4 Sew the binding strips end to end to make a continuous binding. Bind the edges of the quilt.

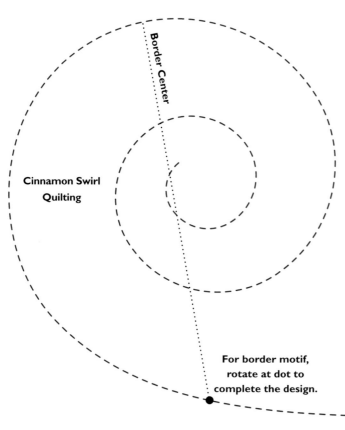

Border Center

Cinnamon Swirl
Quilting

For border motif,
rotate at dot to
complete the design.

A

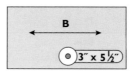

3″ x 3″

B

3″ x 5½″

C

C

3⅜″ x 3⅜″

Center
of Block

Just for Fun

Designed by the *Quiltmaker* magazine staff, made by Shirley Wegert. Border, sash, and binding fabrics from Northcott/Monarch. Modeled by Benjamin Azbell.

This quilt was designed by the *Quiltmaker* magazine staff for a community quiltmaking day in support of Project Linus, a wonderful international pro bono organization that provides handmade quilts, blankets, and comforters for seriously ill or traumatized children. To learn more about Project Linus and other ways that you can make and contribute quilts for children in need, see pages 4 and 80.

QUILT SIZES:	Crib/Wall Quilt	Twin Comforter (shown)
	38" × 47"	66" × 87"
FINISHED BLOCK SIZE:		
7" × 7"		
YARDAGE		
Blue Print	¾ yard	2½ yards
border sides*	2 at 5½" × 39½"	2 at 5½" × 79½"
border top/bottom*	2 at 5½" × 40½"	2 at 5½" × 68½"
Green Print	½ yard	¾ yard
double-fold binding	5 at 2¼" × 40"	9 at 2¼" × 38"
Multiprint	½ yard**	1⅞ yards
sashes***	3 at 3½" × 28½"	7 at 3½" × 56½"
Assorted Prints	scraps	scraps
foundation piecing	patches 1–9	patches 1–9
Backing	1¾ yards	5½ yards
panel[s]	1 at 42" × 51"	2 at 36" × 91"
sleeve (optional)	1 at 9" × 38"	none for this size
Batting	42" × 51"	70" × 91"

*An extra 2" have been added to the length for insurance.
**For directional prints parallel to the selvages, you will need ⅞ yard.
***Seam allowance is included in the length, but no extra has been added for insurance.

Getting Started

For more detailed directions on quiltmaking, see Quilting Basics (pages 76–79).

Directions are for both the crib/wall quilt and the twin comforter. Information specific to the twin size is given in brackets [ ].

The blocks for this quilt are varied and fun, with center patches made from novelty prints. Directional fabrics with the 3½"-wide stripes running parallel to the selvages were used for the sashes, but nondirectional fabrics would also work well. Yardages are included for both.

For each block, select one novelty print for foundation patch 1. Use a second fabric for patches 2–5. Select a third fabric for patches 6–9. Make sure the fabrics contrast well.

Making the Top

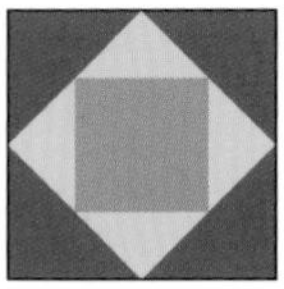

1 Make 16 [64] copies of the foundation pattern. You can either trace the pattern or use an accurate photocopy machine. Compare your copies with the original to ensure accuracy.

Block
Make 16 [64]

2 In numerical order, foundation piece patches 1–9. Trim extra fabric and paper along the outer line. Join 4 [8] blocks to make a row. Sew a row and sash

together, matching centers and ends. Press the seam allowances toward the sash. Repeat to add the remaining rows and sashes.

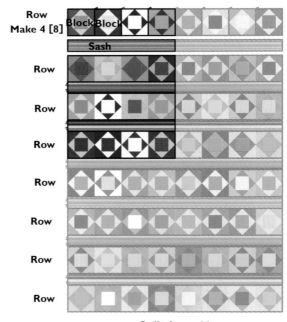

Quilt Assembly
Crib/wall quilt is shown in darker colors.
Twin comforter includes the complete diagram.

3 For the squared border, add the side strips first. Press the seam allowances away from the quilt center and trim any excess length. Add the top and bottom strips in the same way.

4 Remove the paper foundations.

Quilting and Finishing

1 In the border, mark a line 1½″ out from the row seams, as shown, and another line 1½″ out from this first marked line. Mark a third line down the center of each sash.

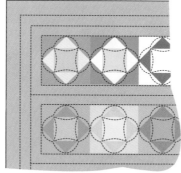

Quilting Placement

2 Layer the backing, batting, and quilt top. Baste the layers together.

3 By eye, quilt the arcs as shown in the Quilting Placement diagram. (For machine quilting, these are continuous stitching lines within each block). Quilt the rows in-the-ditch. Quilt the marked lines in the sashes and border.

4 Sew the binding strips end to end to make a continuous binding. Bind the edges of the quilt.

5 To display the quilt on a wall, sew a sleeve to the backing.

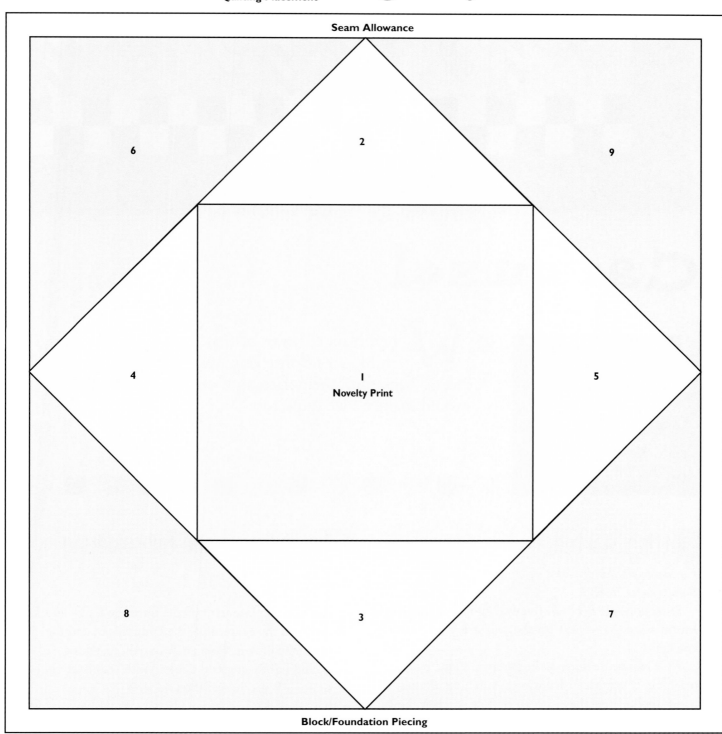

Seam Allowance

6

2

9

4

1
Novelty Print

5

8

3

7

Block/Foundation Piecing

Carousel

**Designed by
Nancy S. Brown,
made by Mickie Swall.
Fabrics from
Hi-Fashion Fabrics,
Inc., and Robert
Kaufman.**

When Nancy Brown of Oakland, California, was a child, her favorite ride was the carousel. It still brings back fond memories, so she thought the carousel would make a nice quilt, too.

Getting Started

For more detailed directions on quiltmaking, see Quilting Basics (pages 76–79).

Directions are for both the wall and the crib quilt. Information that differs for the crib size is given in brackets [ ].

This pattern features satin-stitch appliqué by machine. If you prefer handwork, stitching around hand-appliqué patches with an outline stitch will give a similar look to the quilt.

Satin Stitching and Embroidering the Blocks

1 To make a placement guide, trace the C, D, and E patches, the center line, the embroidery, and the satin-stitched mane. Fold an A in half, matching 12″ sides, and lightly crease the fold. With stabilizer under A, center a B patch over the fold, and sew in place with a ⅛″-wide satin stitch. Use your placement guide to position a C patch, and satin stitch it in place.

(continued on page 22.)

Muted colors are reminiscent of the now faded carousels of yesteryear. Thread colors that match each fabric soften the outline.

Materials and Cutting

FINISHED QUILT SIZES:
  Wall Quilt (shown): 54″ × 22½″
  Crib Quilt: 42″ × 49½″

FINISHED BLOCK SIZE: 12″ × 10½″

YARDAGE	Wall Quilt (shown)	Crib Quilt
White Solid	⅜ yard	½ yard
strips	4 at 2″ × 40″	6 at 2″ × 40″
Black Solid	⅜ yard	½ yard
strips	4 at 2″ × 40″	6 at 2″ × 40″
Black and White Stripe	½ yard	½ yard
	4 B	9 B
Blue Print	1⅝ yards	1⅜ yards
inner border sides*	2 at 1½″ × 19″	2 at 1½″ × 46″
inner border top/bottom*	2 at 1½″ × 52½″	2 at 1½″ × 40½″
Red Print	1⅔ yards	1½ yards
outer border sides*	2 at 2½″ × 21″	2 at 2½″ × 48″
outer border top/bottom*	2 at 2½″ × 56½″	2 at 2½″ × 44½″
Yellow Print	½ yard	½ yard
double-fold binding	5 at 2¼″ × 36″	6 at 2¼″ × 35″
Scrap Requirements for the Blocks		
Background	4 at 12″ × 13½″	9 at 12″ × 13½″
from each fabric	1 A**	1 A**
Tail	4 at 3½″ × 3½″	9 at 3½″ × 3½″
from each fabric	1 C	1 C
Body	4 at 8″ × 10″	9 at 8″ × 10″
from each fabric	1 D	1 D
Saddle	4 at 2½″ × 2½″	9 at 2½″ × 2½″
from each fabric	1 E	1 E
Backing	1¾ yards	2¾ yards
cut panels	1 at 27″ × 58″	2 at 28″ × 46″
sleeve	1 at 9″ × 54″	none for this size
Batting	27″ × 58″	46″ × 54″

SUPPLIES: stabilizer for appliqué, black embroidery floss

*An extra 2″ have been added to the length for insurance.   **Trim to 11″ × 12½″ after appliqué is complete.

Mark the facial features and the mane on a D. Then position and stitch the D and E patches. Satin stitch lines for the mane.

2 Repeat Step 1 for all the blocks, positioning the ponies at different levels—just as you'd see them on an amusement park carousel. Remove the stabilizer. Trim each A patch to 11" tall × 12½" wide. Trim away any fabrics underneath the appliqué patches that show through.

3 Use 3 strands of floss to embroider each pony's eye, nose, and mouth.

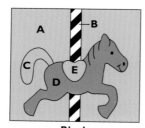

**Block
Make 4 [9]
(varying placement of horse)**

Rather Not Hand Embroider?

Draw each pony's facial features with a wide-line fabric marker, such as a Pigma 08.

▾ Making the Sashes

1 For strip-pieced sashes, sew the white and black strips together to make the bands.

2 Cut the bands into 2" units.

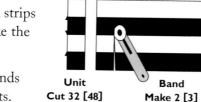

**Unit
Cut 32 [48]**

**Band
Make 2 [3]**

Keep a Sharp Point

If you use sheets of paper as a stabilizer, you'll need to replace your needle periodically because stitching through the paper will dull its tip. You'll know it's time to change needles when the quality of the stitches begins to deteriorate.

▾ Completing Your Quilt Top

1 Refer to the Sash Row diagram to join 8 [6] strip-pieced units end to end. Repeat. Join to make a sash row. Make 1 [3] more sash rows like this.

2 Arrange the blocks for a pleasing mix of colors. Sew 4 [3] blocks together to make each row.

3 Join the sash and block rows as shown.

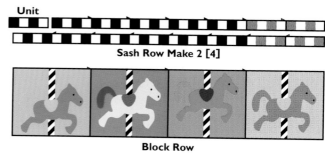

Sash Row Make 2 [4]

**Block Row
Make 1 [3]
Wall quilt includes the complete diagram.
Crib quilt is shown in color.**

4 For squared borders, sew the border strips to the quilt in this order: inner side strips, inner top and bottom, outer sides, outer top and bottom. Trim excess length each time.

▾ Quilting and Finishing

1 If you want to mark the echo quilting in the A patches, do so now, placing the lines approximately 1" apart.

2 Layer and baste the backing, batting, and quilt top.

3 Quilt in-the-ditch the ponies, saddles, and poles. Echo quilt around each pony, stopping at the pole. Grid quilt the sashes as shown. Quilt the borders in-the-ditch.

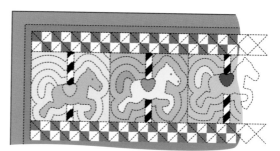

4 Sew the binding strips end to end to make a continuous binding. Bind the edges of the quilt.

5 To display the wall quilt, sew a sleeve to the backing.

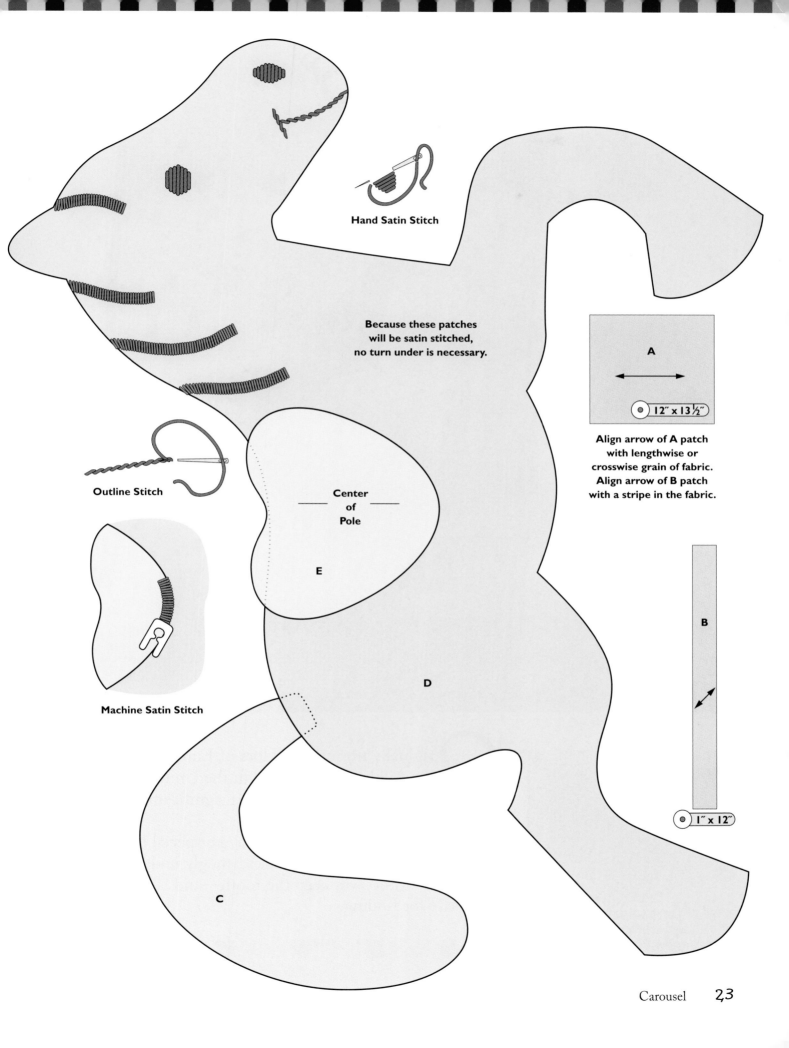

Hand Satin Stitch

Because these patches
will be satin stitched,
no turn under is necessary.

A

⊙ 12″ x 13½″

Align arrow of A patch
with lengthwise or
crosswise grain of fabric.
Align arrow of B patch
with a stripe in the fabric.

Outline Stitch

Center
of
Pole

E

B

Machine Satin Stitch

D

⊙ 1″ x 12″

C

Tooth Fairy

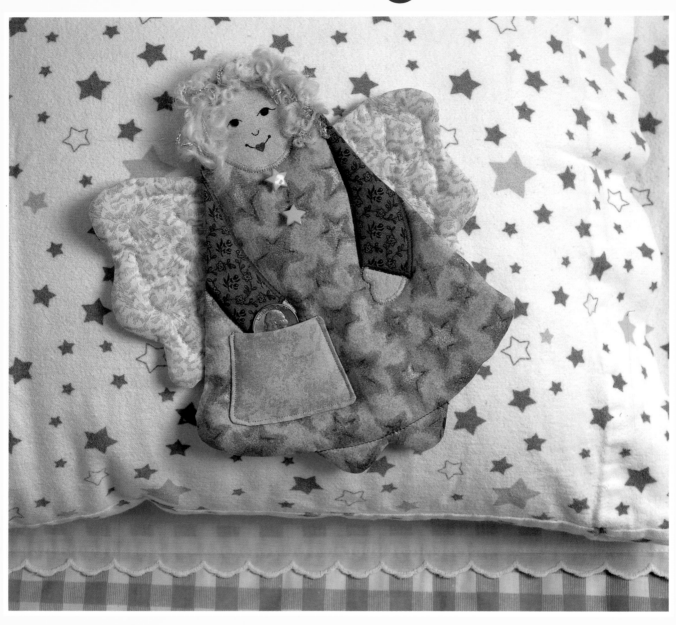

Originally from the folklore of European cultures, the tooth fairy appeared in the United States early in the 1900s and has become a significant nighttime visitor to most households.

Her exchange for the tooth may be special little treats or money. This Tooth Fairy, tucked snugly under the pillow at bedtime, will keep the tooth—and later the gift—safe for finding.

Designed by Carolyn Reardon, made by Peg Spradlin.

Materials and Cutting

TOOTH FAIRY SIZE:

$7\frac{3}{4}'' \times 9''$

Cream Scrap	$5\frac{1}{2}'' \times 17''$
	2 F
Yellow Scrap	$4'' \times 6''$
	2 E
Light Pink Scrap	$3'' \times 6''$
	1 B, 1 C, 1 Cr
Medium Blue Scrap	$8'' \times 20''$
	2 A
Dark Blue Scrap	$4'' \times 5''$
	1 D, 1 Dr
Batting	$10'' \times 14''$
	1 A, 1 F

SUPPLIES: black and red fabric pens, pink crayon, fusible web, 16"–20" of yellow yarn, 2 small buttons

Getting Started

For more detailed directions on quiltmaking, see Quilting Basics (pages 76–79).

This pattern features satin stitch appliqué by machine. If you wish to appliqué by hand instead, add $\frac{3}{16}''$ turn-under to patches B–Dr.

Making the Tooth Fairy

1 Trace the patches on the right sides of the light pink and dark blue scraps. Place the B pattern under the pink fabric and use fabric pens to trace the facial features. Follow the manufacturer's directions to add fusible web to these scraps. Cut out patches B–Dr. Position and fuse these patches on the right side of A. Color in rosy cheeks on the face with a pink crayon.

2 Satin stitch these patches in place. We've used a thread color similar to the fabric color of each patch. Remove stabilizer when stitching is complete.

3 Mark the position for the E patch. Mark the quilting motif on 1 F.

4 For the figure: Place the appliquéd A and the plain A, right sides together, on top of the batting A patch. Pin the 3 layers together. Batting side down, sew around the shape, backstitching at the dots. Trim the batting close to

the stitching and clip the fabric at inside corners and curves. Turn right side out and sew the opening closed.

5 For the wings: Follow the same procedure using the 2 F's.

6 For the pocket: Stitch around the E's, with right sides together, backstitching at the dots. Clip corners, turn right side out and press. Sew the opening closed.

Quilting and Finishing

1 Quilt in-the-ditch just outside the satin stitches of B–Dr. Quilt the curved line at the bottom of the skirt to shape Tooth Fairy's feet.

2 Position the pocket and stitch $\frac{1}{8}''$ inside the edge along the sides and bottom through all layers, backstitching at both top corners.

3 Loop the yarn as you go and arrange and tack curls in place around her head, hand sewing through just the top fabric and batting. Add buttons to her dress.

4 Quilt the wings as marked. Tack them in place through the back and batting.

5 Now she's ready to sleep under a pillow, trading the little tooth in her pocket for a morning treasure.

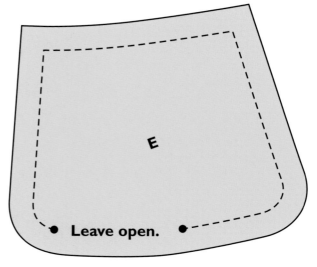

E

Leave open.

Tooth Fairy   25

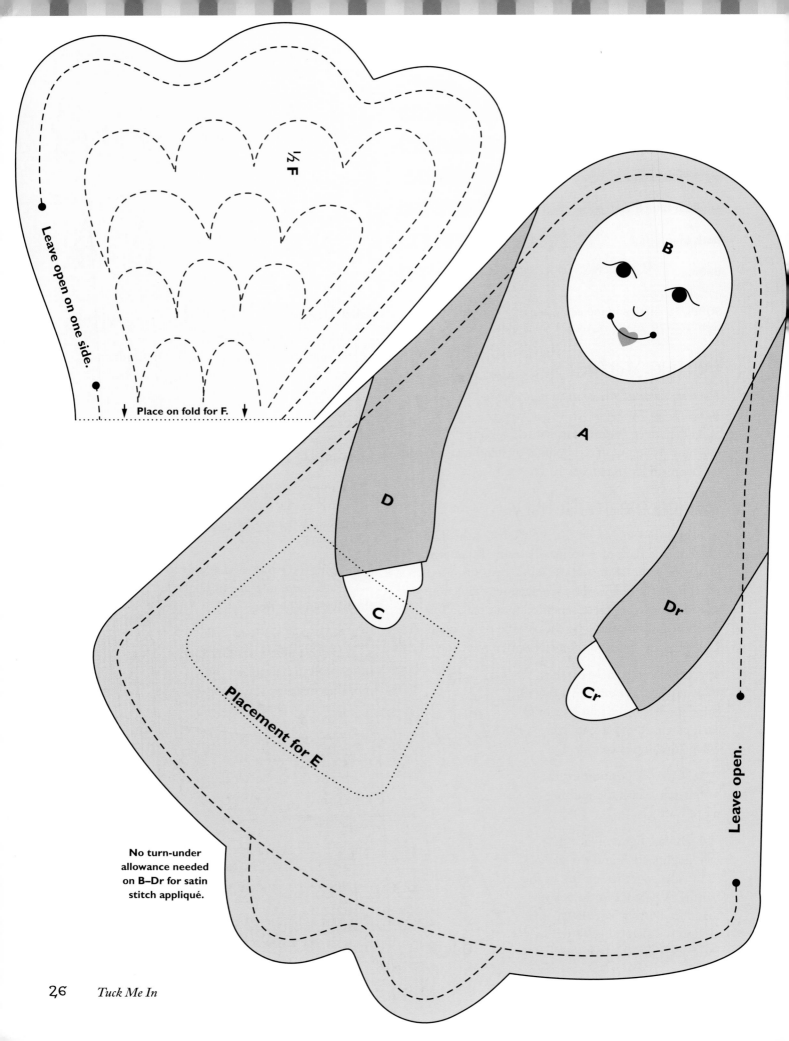

½F

Leave open on one side.

Place on fold for F.

B

A

D

Dr

C

Cr

Placement for E

Leave open.

No turn-under
allowance needed
on B–Dr for satin
stitch appliqué.

Leap Frog

These easy to cut and sew frogs are perfect for any growing tadpole. Pull out your favorite green fabrics, and leap to it.

Made by Carolee Miller. Border and background fabrics from P&B Textiles.

QUILT SIZES:	Wide/Long Twin	Nap/Wall Quilt Comforter (shown)
	73″ × 93″	40″ × 60″
FINISHED BLOCK SIZE:		
10″ × 10″		
YARDAGE		
Green and Teal Scraps	39 at 8″ × 9″**	15 at 8″ × 9″**
from each fabric	2 A, 2 D, 2 E, 1 F	2 A, 2 D, 2 E, 1 F
Light Teal Print	1¾ yards	1¾ yards
	30 A, 45 B, 45 Br, 30 C, 30 E, 15 G	30 A, 45 B, 45 Br, 30 C, 30 E, 15 G
Medium Teal Print	2⅝ yards	none for this size
	48 A, 72 B, 72 Br, 48 C, 48 E, 24 G	
Dark Teal Multiprint	2½ yards	1⅝ yards
border 1 sides	2 at 5½″ × 50½″***	2 at 5½″ × 52½″*
border 1 top/bottom	2 at 5½″ × 40½″***	2 at 5½″ × 42½″*
border 3 sides*	2 at 2″ × 82½″	none for this size
border 3 top/bottom*	2 at 2″ × 65½″	none for this size
Blue Print	⅔ yard	½ yard
double-fold binding	10 at 2¼″ × 37″	6 at 2¼″ × 38″
Black Multiprint	2½ yards	none for this size
border 4 sides*	2 at 5½″ × 85½″	
border 4 top/bottom*	2 at 5½″ × 75½″	
Backing	5¾ yards	2⅝ yards
panels	2 at 39″ × 97″	2 at 33″ × 44″
sleeve	none for this size	1 at 9″ × 40″
Batting	77″ × 97″	44″ × 64″

SUPPLIES: white and black embroidery floss, blue embroidery floss (optional)

*An extra 2″ have been added to the length for insurance.
**You'll need scraps at least 10″ × 10″ for directional prints.
***Seam allowance is included in the length, but no extra has been added for insurance.

▽ Getting Started

For more detailed directions on quiltmaking, see Quilting Basics (pages 76–79).

Directions are for both the wide/long twin comforter and the nap/wall quilt. Information that differs for the nap/wall quilt is given in brackets [ ].

Cutting directions are provided for the best use of directional and nondirectional prints.

Satin Stitch   Running Stitch   Outline Stitch

French Knot

▽ Cutting the Patches

1 For the B/Br patches, fold both teal fabrics in half to cut both kinds of patches at once.

2 To cut the patches for each frog, use the rotary cutting dimensions on page 31 to make templates for A and D–F, and follow the appropriate cutting diagram. For directional prints, change the grainline of F to run the length of the patch.

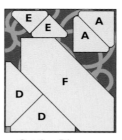

**Cutting Diagram
for Nondirectional Prints**

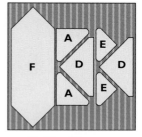

**Cutting Diagram
for Directional Prints**

Making and Embroidering the Blocks

1 The piecing of the Y and Z blocks is the same; only the background fabric differs. Make 15 [15] Y blocks and 24 [0] Z blocks, pressing the seam allowances in the directions shown.

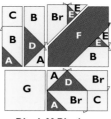
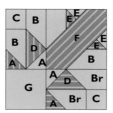

Block Y Piecing
Make 15 [15]

Block Z
Make 24 [0]

2 Outline stitch each frog's eyes with 3 strands of white embroidery floss. Satin stitch the pupils with black floss and then fill in with white.

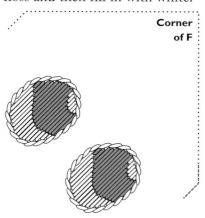

Corner
of F

3 If you wish, embroider flies on a few G patches. (We used blue floss for our flies.) Satin stitch the bodies, make French knots for the eyes, outline stitch the wings, and sew a running stitch for the tails.

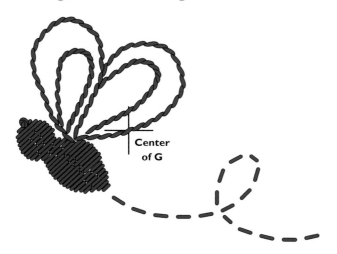

Center
of G

Assembling the Quilt Top

1 Refer to the Quilt Assembly diagram. To make the center portion, turn the frogs in one direction and sew the Y blocks together to make 5 rows of 3 blocks each. Press the seam allowances of every other row in the same direction. Join the rows and press the seam allowances in one direction.

2 For squared borders, sew the border 1 side strips to the center portion. [Trim excess length.] Then sew the top and bottom border 1 strips to the quilt [and trim]. If you are making the nap/wall quilt, go to Step 1 of Quilting and Finishing.

3 For border 2, orient and join the blocks as shown. Sew the borders first to the sides of the quilt and then to the top and bottom.

4 Sew the border 3 side strips to the quilt. Trim excess length. Sew the border 3 top and bottom strips to the quilt; trim. Join the border 4 strips in the same order.

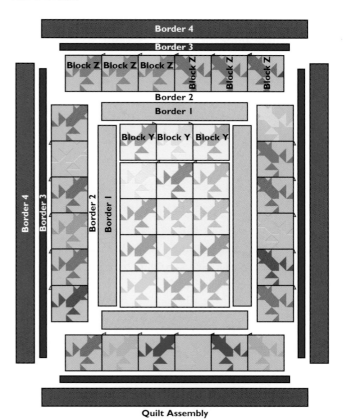

Quilt Assembly

Nap/wall quilt is shown in lighter colors.
Twin comforter includes the complete diagram.

Quilting and Finishing

1 Fold borders 1 and 4 [border 1] in half lengthwise, and lightly press. Trace the *Pond Ripple* quilting. Match the centers and align the reference dots with the block seamlines. Mark borders 1 and 4 [border 1]. Use freehand flowing lines to connect the motifs in each corner.

Quilting Placement

2 Layer the backing, batting, and quilt top. Baste the layers together.

3 Outline quilt around the frogs as shown. Meander quilt the F patches. Quilt the border motifs as marked.

4 Sew the binding strips end to end to make a continuous binding. Bind the edges of the quilt.

5 To display the wall quilt, sew a sleeve to the backing.

Camouflage Your Colors

Are you new to quilting? Uneven stitches are less noticeable when your thread color matches your backing fabric. Using a busy print for the backing is another way to disguise less-than-perfect stitches.

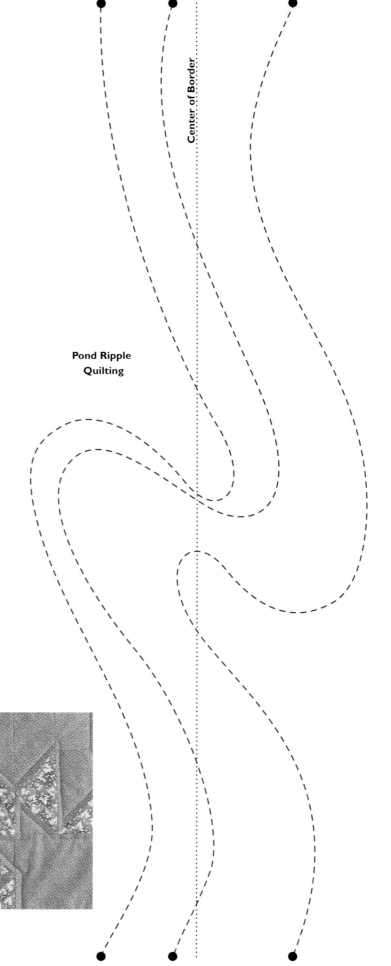

Pond Ripple Quilting

Center of Border

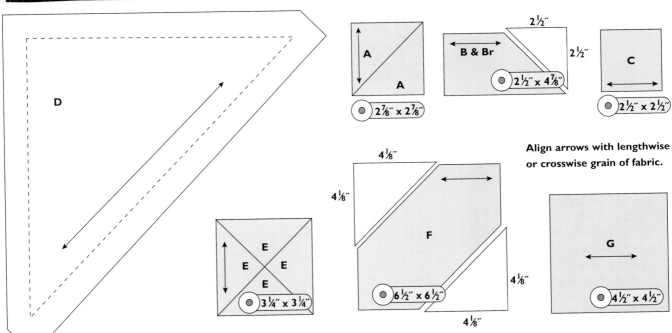

A — $2\frac{7}{8}'' \times 2\frac{7}{8}''$

B & Br — $2\frac{1}{2}'' \times 4\frac{7}{8}''$, $2\frac{1}{2}''$, $2\frac{1}{2}''$

C — $2\frac{1}{2}'' \times 2\frac{1}{2}''$

Align arrows with lengthwise or crosswise grain of fabric.

E — $3\frac{1}{4}'' \times 3\frac{1}{4}''$

F — $6\frac{1}{2}'' \times 6\frac{1}{2}''$, $4\frac{1}{8}''$, $4\frac{1}{8}''$, $4\frac{1}{8}''$, $4\frac{1}{8}''$

G — $4\frac{1}{2}'' \times 4\frac{1}{2}''$

Little Mittens

L ittle *Mittens* is a great size to wrap around those young'uns after a good romp in the snow or just to display on a wall.

Designed by the *Quiltmaker* magazine staff and made by Shirley Wegert. Background fabrics from RJR Fashion Fabrics and Northcott/Monarch. Modeled by Janice Dickman.

Materials and Cutting

QUILT SIZE:	Crib/Wall Quilt
	36" × 47"
FINISHED BLOCK SIZE:	
8" × 8"	
YARDAGE	
Dark Blue Print	⅜ yard
double-fold binding	5 at 2¼" × 39"
Medium Blue Print	1 yard
	31 F
Bright Prints (mitten pairs)	4 fat quarters
from each print	
bias strip	1 at 1¼" × 22"
	1 B, 1 Br, 1 D, 1 Dr
Bright Prints (mitten single)	4 at 6" × 12"
from each print	1 B or Br, 1 D, 1 Dr
Light Prints (mitten pairs)	4 at 3" × 10"
from each print	2 C
Light Prints (mitten single)	4 at 3" × 5"
from each print	1 C
White Print	1⅝ yards
	12 A*, 20 E*
Backing	1⅞ yards
panel	1 at 40" × 51"
sleeve (optional)	1 at 9" × 36"
Batting	40" × 51"

*After the appliqué is complete, trim the A's to 8½" × 8½" and the E's to 3½" × 3½".

Getting Started

For more detailed directions on quiltmaking, including making bias strips, see Quilting Basics (pages 76–79).

We selected bright fabrics to warm the spirits. For each mitten, pick two fabrics of the same color, a dark fabric for the hand and a lighter one for the cuff.

Appliquéing the Mittens

1 Each pair of mittens is connected with a bias strip "string." Cut a bias strip from each fat quarter; then prepare the bias strips and B–Dr patches using your preferred method.

2 Use the Quilt Assembly diagram as your guide to center by eye the B's, Br's, and C's, and blindstitch to A in alphabetical order. Leave a 1" opening at the bottom of the cuff of each pair of mittens to insert the end of the string. Likewise, position and appliqué D/Dr's on all but 4 E patches. Center the appliqué and trim the A and E patches as indicated in the yardage.

Assembling the Quilt Top

1 Make the rows. Press the seam allowances toward the F blocks. Sew the rows together, and then press the seam allowances as shown.

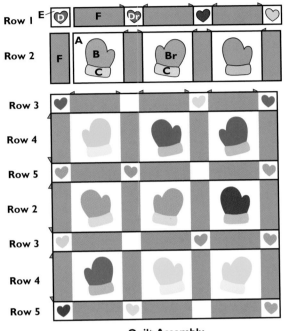

Quilt Assembly

2 Match each bias strip to a mitten pair, loop the strings in the plain E's, and tuck the ends into the openings of the cuffs. Trim the lengths as needed. Blindstitch the strings in place, and then blindstitch the openings closed.

Quilting and Finishing

1 Trace the *Whispering Pines* quilting and mark 3 motifs in each F, following the Quilting Placement guide.

Quilting Placement

2 Layer the backing, batting, and quilt top. Baste the layers together.

3 Quilt in-the-ditch the patches and strings and then quilt the marked motifs. For continuous-line machine quilting, first quilt the lines shown in white and then quilt the lines shown in blue.

4 Sew the binding strips end to end to make a continuous binding. Bind the edges of the quilt.

5 To display the quilt on a wall, sew a sleeve to the backing.

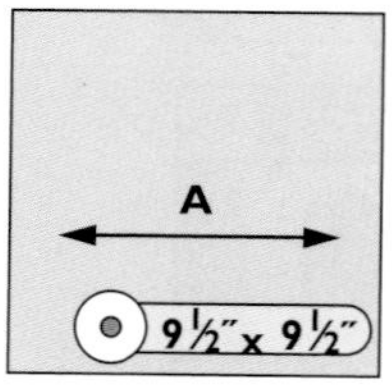

A

$9\frac{1}{2}$" x $9\frac{1}{2}$"

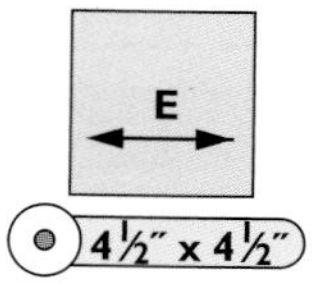

E

$4\frac{1}{2}$" x $4\frac{1}{2}$"

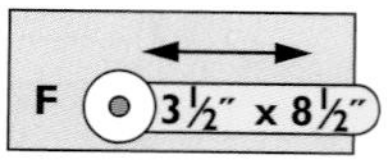

F $3\frac{1}{2}$" x $8\frac{1}{2}$"

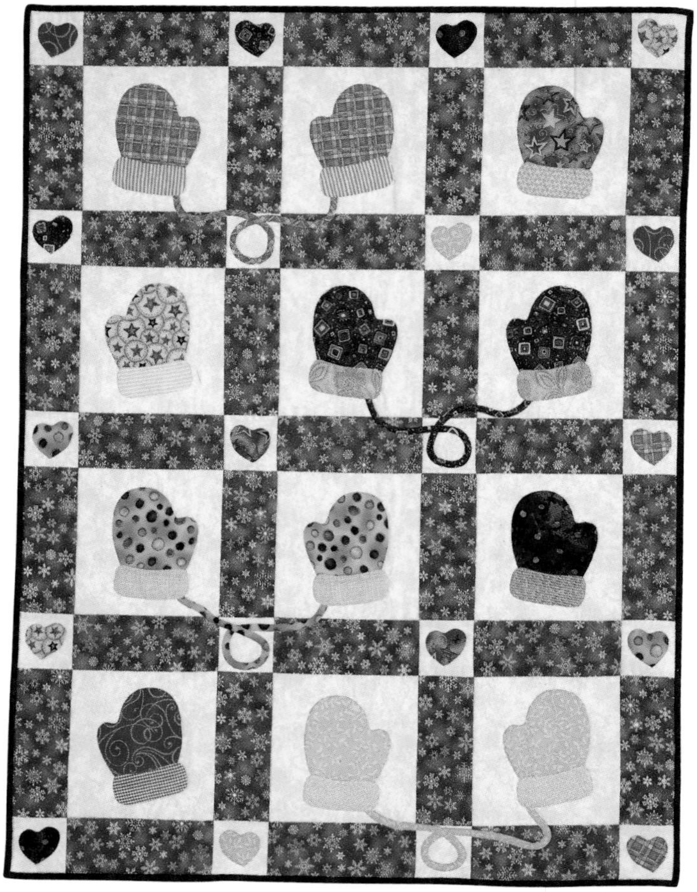

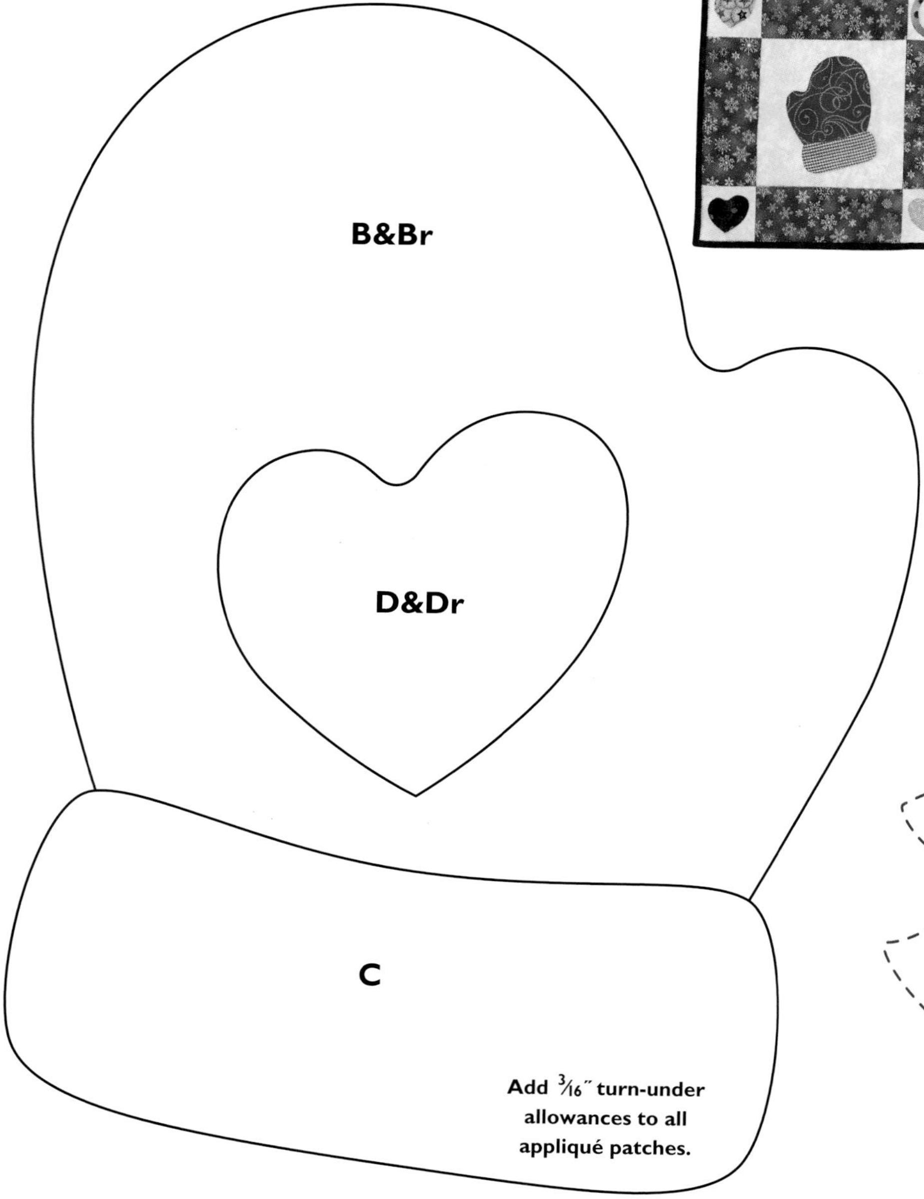

B&Br

D&Dr

C

Add $\frac{3}{16}$" turn-under allowances to all appliqué patches.

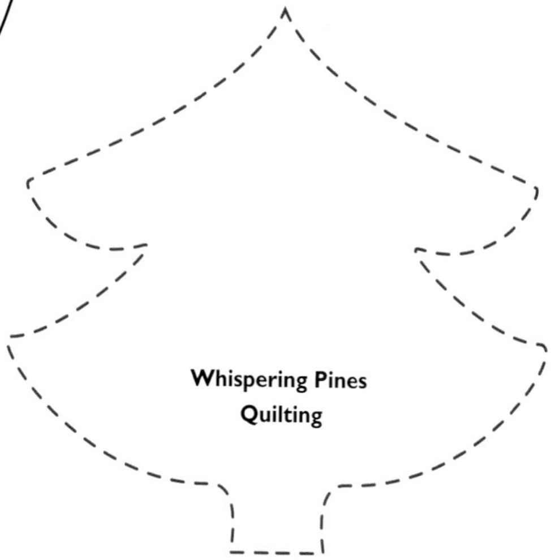

Whispering Pines Quilting

Parade of Shapes

Colleen Harvey of Nederland, Colorado, loves working with simple geometric shapes. She designed this arrangement of rows, which are showcased by simple sashing. Seeing the shapes march across the quilt reminded her of a parade.

Designed by Colleen Harvey, made by Mickie Swall. Fabrics from Quilting Treasures and Timeless Treasures.

QUILT SIZES:	Twin Comforter (shown)	Sofa Quilt
	66″ × 90″	54″ × 72″
FINISHED BLOCK SIZE:		
6″ × 6″		
YARDAGE		
Dark Blue Print	2 yards	1²⁄₃ yards
sashes*	4 at 3½″ × 68½″	3 at 3½″ × 56½″
double-fold binding	5 at 2¼″ × 68″	5 at 2¼″ × 56″
strip	1 at 3½″ × 40″	1 at 3½″ × 40″
	10 B, 1 C, 1 Cr	8 B, 1 C, 1 Cr
Medium Blue Print	2 yards	1²⁄₃ yards
sash*	1 at 3½″ × 68½″	1 at 3½″ × 56½″
strips	2 at 2″ × 40″	2 at 2″ × 40″
	11 F, 11 G	9 F
Medium-Light Blue Print	⅛ yard	⅛ yard
strip	1 at 3½″ × 40″	1 at 3½″ × 40″
Teal Print	⅝ yard	⅜ yard
strips	2 at 2½″ × 40″	2 at 2½″ × 40″
	5 D, 6 H	4 D
Dark Green Print	⅝ yard	⅝ yard
strips	2 at 2½″ × 40″	2 at 2½″ × 40″
strips	2 at 2″ × 40″	2 at 2″ × 40″
	6 E, 11 F	5 E, 9 F
Light Green Print	2 yards	1²⁄₃ yards
sash*	1 at 3½″ × 68½″	1 at 3½″ × 56½″
strip	1 at 2½″ × 40″	1 at 2½″ × 40″
	11 F, 5 H	9 F
Yellow Print	2 yards	1²⁄₃ yards
sash*	1 at 3½″ × 68½″	1 at 3½″ × 56½″
strips	2 at 3½″ × 40″	2 at 3½″ × 40″
strips	2 at 2″ × 40″	2 at 2″ × 40″
	16 A, 6 D, 5 H	13 A, 5 D
Dark Orange Print	2 yards	1²⁄₃ yards
sash*	1 at 3½″ × 68½″	1 at 3½″ × 56½″
strip	1 at 6½″ × 66½″	1 at 6½″ × 54½″
Medium Orange Print	2 yards	1²⁄₃ yards
sash*	1 at 3½″ × 68½″	1 at 3½″ × 56½″
	6 D	
Red Print	1 yard	1 yard
strips	2 at 2″ × 40″	2 at 2″ × 40″
	11 B, 5 E, 11 F	9 B, 4 E, 9 F
Dark Purple Print	2 yards	⅛ yard
sash*	1 at 3½″ × 68½″	none for this size
strip	1 at 2½″ × 40″	1 at 2½″ × 40″
	11 G	
Medium Purple Print	2 yards	1²⁄₃ yards
sash*	1 at 3½″ × 68½″	1 at 3½″ × 56½″
strips	2 at 3½″ × 40″	2 at 3½″ × 40″
	5 D, 6 H	
Backing	5⅝ yards	3½ yards
panels	2 at 36″ × 94″	2 at 39″ × 58″
Batting	70″ × 94″	58″ × 76″

*An extra 2″ have been added to the length for insurance.

Getting Started

For more detailed directions on quiltmaking, see Quilting Basics (pages 76–79).

Directions are for both the twin comforter and the sofa quilt. Information specific to the sofa size is given in brackets [ ].

Piecing the Units and the U, V, Y, and Z Blocks

1 Refer to the strip-piecing diagrams and press the seam allowances for each band as shown. Sew together the 2½″ × 40″ strips to make bands A and B. Sew together the 2″ × 40″ strips to make the band C's. Sew together the 3½″ × 40″ strips to make bands D and E. Cut each band into units as shown.

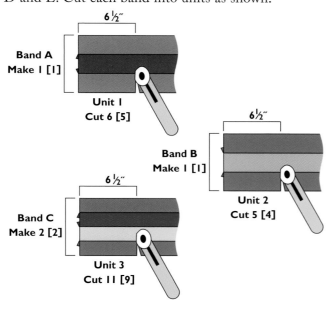

Band A
Make 1 [1]

6½″

Unit 1
Cut 6 [5]

Band B
Make 1 [1]

6½″

Unit 2
Cut 5 [4]

Band C
Make 2 [2]

6½″

Unit 3
Cut 11 [9]

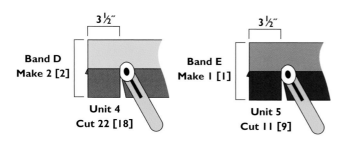

3½″

Band D
Make 2 [2]

Unit 4
Cut 22 [18]

3½″

Band E
Make 1 [1]

Unit 5
Cut 11 [9]

2 Follow the block diagram to sew together the unit 4's to make the U blocks.

Unit 4

Unit 4

Block U
Make 11 [9]

3 Join the F's to make the V blocks. Join the H's to make the Y and Z blocks.

F
F
F
F

Block V Piecing
Make 11 [9]

H
H

Block Y
Make 6 [0]

H
H

Block Z
Make 5 [0]

Appliquéing the S, T, W, and X Blocks

1 Fold the yellow and teal D patches in half both ways, and lightly crease the centers. Prepare the E's for appliqué with your favorite method and fold in half both ways to crease the centers. Match centers and blindstitch the E's in place.

D
E

Block S
Make 6 [5]

D
E

Block T
Make 5 [4]

2 For the twin comforter, fold the medium orange and medium purple D's in half and crease to mark the centers of the edges.

3 Prepare the curved edges of the G's for appliqué; the straight edges will be sewn into the seam allowances. Fold the straight edges in half and crease to mark centers. Match centers and align raw edges, then blindstitch the curved edges of the G's on the D's.

D
G
G

Block W
Make 6 [0]

D
G
G

Block X
Make 5 [0]

Making the Rows

1 Trace the A patch and center line to make a template. Measure in 1″ from both edges of the top left corner of the 6½″-wide dark

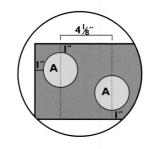

4⅛″
1″
A
1″
A
1″

orange strip. Trace an A patch as shown. Mark the remaining A patch placement, centering each A 4⅛" apart and 1" in from the long edges. For a more casual look, position the A's by eye.

2 Prepare the A's for appliqué, and blindstitch them in place.

Blind Stitch

3 Refer to the Quilt Assembly diagram to sew together the units and blocks as needed to make row 2 and rows 4–8 [10]. Press the seam allowances for each row as shown.

4 Join the B's, C, and Cr patches to make row 3. Press the seam allowances as shown.

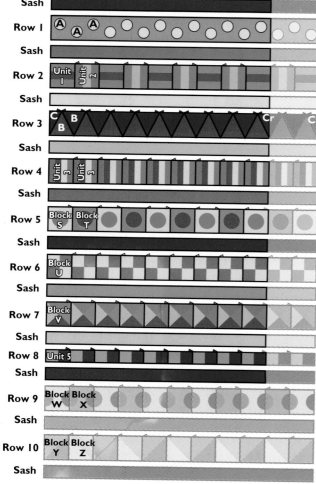

Quilt Assembly
Sofa quilt is shown in darker colors.
Twin comforter includes the complete diagram.

Completing the Top

1 Measure the length of each row. Using the shortest measurement, trim each sash to this length.

2 Sew together the sash and row 1, matching the centers and ends, easing any fullness as needed. Press the seam allowances toward the sash. Repeat to add the remaining sashes and rows.

Quilting and Finishing

1 You can do the quilting without marking the quilt top. If you prefer to mark, trace the E patch on template plastic to make a quilting template. Using the Quilting Placement diagram for reference, mark the small circles with the A patch template from Making the Rows, Step 1. Mark the large circles with the E patch template as shown. Use the patchwork as a guide to mark the straight lines.

2 Layer the backing, batting, and quilt top. Baste the layers together.

3 Outline quilt the sashes ¼" in from the seamlines, and then quilt the motifs. If you are machine quilting, quilt the motifs in continuous lines.

Quilting Placement

4 Sew the binding strips end to end to make a continuous binding. Bind the edges of the quilt.

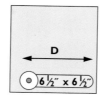

D
6½" x 6½"

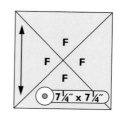

F
F   F
F
7¼" x 7¼"

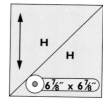

H
H
6⅞" x 6⅞"

A

Center

Add ³⁄₁₆″ turn-under
allowances to A.

Modeled by Alexus Nicole and Austin Dewitt

Place on fold for B.

½ B

C&Cr

Add ³⁄₁₆″ turn-under allowances to all appliqué patches.

E

G

Seam Allowance for G

Pure and Simple

A pair of matching woven-loop potholders that Teresa Minder of Rhinelander, Wisconsin, bought at a winter carnival inspired this one-patch design. When placed side by side as mirror images of each other, the potholders made a pretty design for a child's quilt. Teresa chose pure colors in bright prints to give the quilt sparkle.

**Designed and made by
Teresa Minder.
Modeled by
Andy Wilcoxon and
Danielle Garcia.**

Materials and Cutting

QUILT SIZE:

	Wall Quilt
	61" × 61"

FINISHED BLOCK SIZE:

27½" × 27½"

YARDAGE

Red Print	2 yards
border sides*	2 at 3½" × 57½"
border top/bottom*	2 at 3½" × 63½"
double-fold binding	5 at 2¼" × 54"
	80 A
Green Print	¾ yard
	80 A
Yellow Print	¾ yard
	80 A
Blue Print	¾ yard
	80 A
Purple Print	¾ yard
	80 A
Backing	4 yards
panels	2 at 33" × 65"
sleeve	1 at 9" × 61"
Batting	65" × 65"

*An extra 2" have been added to the length for insurance.

Getting Started

For more detailed directions on quiltmaking, see Quilting Basics (pages 76–79).

Because the order of the patches varies from row to row, using the strip-piecing method of sewing patches is inefficient. Instead, in this quilt, you get to experience the good old days of quiltmaking by cutting 80 individual patches of each color.

If you fold each fabric in four layers, you'll only need to cut twenty stacks.

Making the Center

1 Lay out the patches following the color placement on the Block Piecing diagram. Join the patches to make 10 rows, pressing the seam allowances of every other row in the same direction. This allows you to nest seams when you attach rows. Join the rows and press all the seam allowances between rows in the same direction. Make 4 blocks.

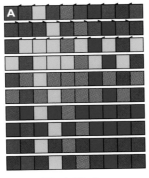

Block Piecing
Make 4

2 Orient the blocks according to the Quilt Assembly diagram, and join them to complete the quilt top.

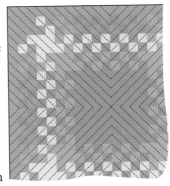

Quilt Assembly

Adding the Squared Border

1 Sew the shorter border strips to opposite sides of the quilt. Press the seam allowances toward the strips and trim any extra length.

2 Add the top and bottom border strips to the quilt. Press and trim as in Step 1.

Quilting and Finishing

1 Layer the backing, batting, and quilt top. Baste the layers together.

2 Use the patchwork as a guide to quilt diagonal lines through the center from corner to corner. As shown in the Quilting Placement diagram, quilt additional lines through each patch and into the border, forming a chevron pattern parallel to the center lines.

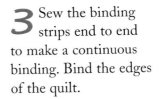

Quilting Placement

3 Sew the binding strips end to end to make a continuous binding. Bind the edges of the quilt.

4 To display the quilt on a wall, sew a sleeve to the backing.

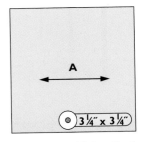

A

3¼" x 3¼"

Align arrow with lengthwise or crosswise grain of fabric.

'Tis a Gift to Be Simple

The beauty of this one-patch quilt lies in the simple way it alternates colors to mimic a weaving. Featuring all the primary and secondary colors except orange, this design makes a lively wall-hanging or a cheery gift for a child.

Stars for Lucas

A collection of cheerful prints was the starting point for this quilt, made for Sherri Bain Driver's great-nephew Lucas. Working with equilateral triangles is fun and much easier than you might imagine.

Designed and made by Sherri Bain Driver. Modeled by Lucas Goodiel.

QUILT SIZES:	Crib/Wall Quilt (shown) 59" × 57"	Long Twin Comforter 64" × 93"
YARDAGE		
White Multiprint	2 yards	2⅞ yards
	24 A, 10 B, 10 Br, 62 C	48 A, 16 B, 16 Br, 92 C
Blue Print	2 yards	2⅝ yards
border 1 sides*	2 at 3" × 54½"	2 at 3" × 85½"
border 1 top/bottom*	2 at 3" × 61½"	2 at 3" × 61½"
Green Print	none for this size	2¾ yards
border 2 sides*		2 at 3" × 90½"
border 2 top/bottom*		2 at 3" × 66½"
Stripe	½ yard	⅔ yard
double-fold binding	7 at 2¼" × 38"	9 at 2¼" × 39"
Print Scrap 1**	10 at 4" × 9"	17 at 4" × 9"
per scrap	3 A	3 A
Print Scrap 2**	10 at 4" × 9"	17 at 4" × 9"
per scrap	3 A	3 A
Print Scrap 3**	10 at 4" × 17"	17 at 4" × 17"
per scrap	6 A	6 A
Print 4**	8 at ⅛ yard	13 at ⅛ yard
per print	12 A	12 A
Print 5**	8 at ¼ yard	13 at ¼ yard
per print	6 C	6 C
Backing	3¾ yards	5⅞ yards
panels	2 at 32" × 61"	2 at 35" × 97"
sleeve	1 at 9" × 59"	none for this size
Batting	61" × 63"	68" × 97"

*An extra 2" have been added to the length for insurance.

**If you want to cut specific motifs in the prints, you may need more fabric.

Getting Started

For more detailed directions on quiltmaking, see Quilting Basics (pages 76–79).

Directions are for both the crib/wall quilt and the long twin comforter. Information that differs for the larger size is given in brackets [ ].

This quilt was made from novelty prints, polka dots, and geometrics in bright, clear colors. Three white print fabrics were used for the background. We simplified the pattern by giving total background yardage as just one white print.

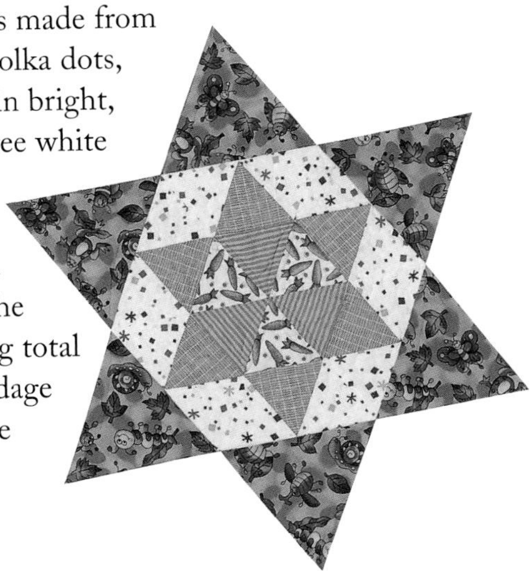

Preparing to Sew

1 For each Y block, choose 4 prints and cut out the A's. Select a fifth print and cut 6 C's for the surrounding large star points.

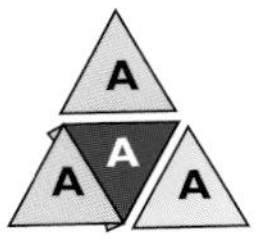

2 Set aside the C's. Cut the A patches for each Z block from 3 scraps and the white multiprint.

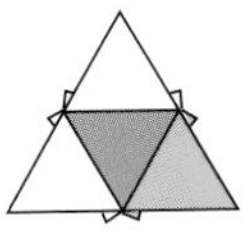

Unit 1 Piecing
Make 3 for each Y Block

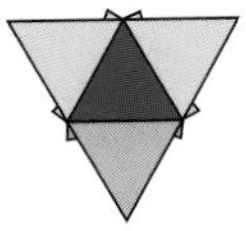

Unit 2
Make 3 for each Y Block

Unit 3
Make 3 for each Z Block

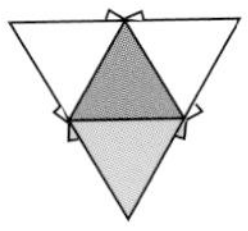

Unit 4
Make 3 for each Z Block

Making the Blocks

Each block is pieced the same, only the fabric placement differs.

1 Follow the diagrams to piece units 1–4. Press the seam allowances away from each center A patch.

2 Join the units to make each half-block Y and each half-block Z. Press open the seam allowances between the units. Do not join the half-blocks.

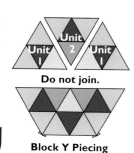

Do not join.

**Block Y Piecing
Make 8 [13]**

Do not join.

**Block Z
Make 2 [4]**

Arranging and Sewing the Rows

1 Follow the Quilt Assembly diagram to place the B's, Br's, C's, and half-blocks. Whenever possible, position the C patches so the straight of the grain is on the outside edge of each row. Sew the patches and blocks together to make the rows. Press the seam allowances of every other row in the same direction.

2 Join the rows. Press open the seams that join the half-blocks; for the other rows, press the seam allowances in one direction.

• = Br **Quilt Assembly**

Crib/wall quilt is shown in darker colors. Long twin comforter includes the complete diagram.

* In the crib/wall quilt, these C patches are white multiprint.

Adding the Squared Border[s]

1 Sew the border 1 strips to the sides of the quilt. Press the seam allowances toward the strips, and trim any extra length.

2 Add the top and bottom strips, trimming and pressing as before. [Sew border 2 strips to the quilt in the same way.]

Quilting and Finishing

1 Layer the backing, batting, and quilt top. Baste the layers together.

2 Follow the diagram to quilt continuous, gently curved lines in the A and C patches. Fill the white multiprint areas with free-motion quilting of meandering lines and randomly placed Critters Charm Tacks.

If you prefer, you can trace the motifs and quilt through the paper. Carefully tear away the paper after quilting. Quilt the border [borders] in-the-ditch, and then quilt parallel lines 1¼" apart. Or quilt around motifs in the print.

Quilting Placement

3 Sew the binding strips end to end to make a continuous binding. Bind the edges of the quilt.

4 To display the wall quilt, sew a sleeve to the backing.

Template Tricks

Trace the templates on see-through plastic. Cut out and then check the accuracy of each template by matching it to the printed pattern. Remake any templates that are inaccurate. Transfer the grainline arrow onto each template. For the A's and C's, the straight of the grain is opposite the trimmed point. If you want a motif to be oriented in a particular way, you may need to ignore grainlines.

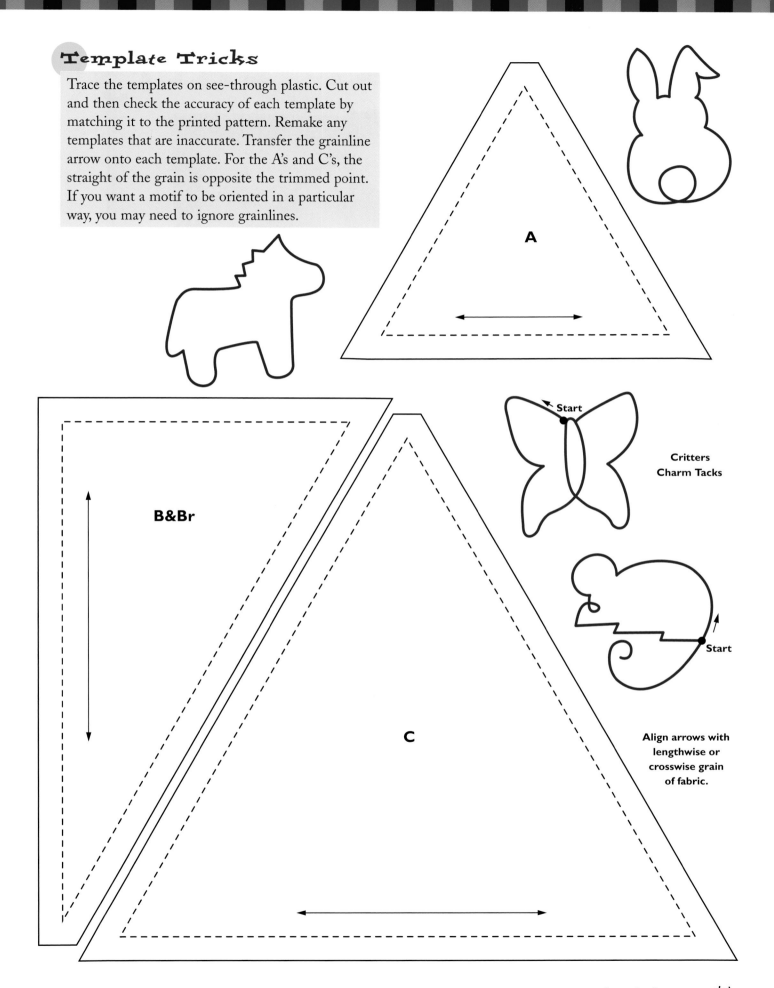

A

B&Br

C

Critters
Charm Tacks

Start

Start

Align arrows with lengthwise or crosswise grain of fabric.

Teddy Bear Party

When Theresa Eisinger's son was born, she made a wholecloth crib quilt with teddy bears and balloons as quilted motifs. Your little one will love this quilt, with its floating balloons in vibrant colors.

Designed by
Theresa Eisinger,
made by Peg Spradlin.
Background fabrics from
P&B Textiles.
Modeled by
Haley Tedstrom.

QUILT SIZES:	Crib/Wall Quilt (shown)	Small Wall Quilt
	40¾" × 40¾"	23¾" × 23¾"
YARDAGE		
White Print	1¾ yards	⅜ yard
	5 A, 4 D, 4 E	1 A, 4 E
Black Print	1⅜ yards	⅔ yard
border sides*	2 at 2½" × 39¼"	2 at 2½" × 22¼"
border top/bottom*	2 at 2½" × 43¼"	2 at 2½" × 26¼"
double-fold binding	5 at 2¼" × 38"	3 at 2¼" × 40"
sashes**	2 at 2½" × 38½"	none for this size
	8 B, 2 C	2 B, 2 C
Brown Prints	scraps	scraps
	3 G, 2 Gr, 5 J	1 G, 1 J
Bright Prints	scraps	scraps
	34 F, 3 H, 2 Hr, 3 I, 2 Ir	5 F, 1 H, 1 I
Backing	2¾ yards	⅞ yard
panels	2 at 23" × 45"	1 at 28" × 28"
sleeve (optional)	1 at 9" × 40"	1 at 9" × 23"
Batting	45" × 45"	28" × 28"

SUPPLIES: assorted colors embroidery floss

*An extra 2" have been added to the length for insurance.
**Seam allowance is included in the length, but no extra has been added for insurance.

Getting Started

For more detailed directions on quiltmaking, see Quilting Basics (pages 76–79).

Directions are for both the crib/wall quilt and the small wall quilt. Information specific to the smaller size is given in brackets [ ].

This design would make a cute friendship quilt. Or friends and family could sign balloons for the new arrival. Though the pattern suggests numbers and placements of balloons, the final look is up to you. If there is "bearly" enough time in your schedule, the smaller quilt makes a great quick gift!

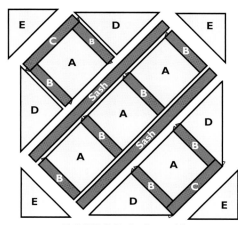

Crib/Wall Quilt Assembly

Making the Top

1 Refer to the appropriate Quilt Assembly diagram to sew the patches together (excluding the E's) to make each [the] diagonal row. Press the seam allowances as shown.

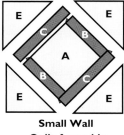

Small Wall Quilt Assembly

2 For the larger size, see Line Up Those B's. Sew the sashes to the middle row, matching centers and ends. Join the rows and press the seam allowances toward the sashes.

Line Up Those B's

To align the B's from row to row in the larger size quilt for a uniform grid, use this pinning technique to mark their placement. First, join the center row and a sash, matching centers and ends. Place pins in the sash at the B seamlines. Match the pins with the B seamlines of the next row, and sew the row and sash together. Repeat for the remaining row and sash.

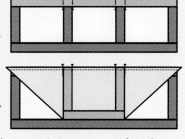

3 Add the E's to all corners.

4 Add the border side strips. Press the seam allowances toward the strips and trim any extra length. Repeat to add the border top and bottom strips.

5 See On the Lighter Side for additional information on appliqué. You do not need to turn under allowances that will be covered by another patch. Use your favorite method to prepare the F–J patches for appliqué. By eye and using the photograph for reference, arrange the patches across the quilt top. Blindstitch each teddy bear, vest, and balloon patch in place in alphabetical order.

6 Use 3 strands of brown floss to outline stitch each leg line. Then use assorted colors of floss to outline stitch the balloon strings. With matching thread color, satin stitch the triangle at the bottom of each balloon.

Quilting and Finishing

1 Trace and cut out the F patch on see-through template plastic. Use the Quilting Placement diagram as a guide to trace around the template to mark the balloon quilting motifs.

2 Layer the backing, batting, and quilt top. Baste the layers together.

3 Quilt the appliqué in-the-ditch, and then quilt the marked motifs. Quilt the border in-the-ditch, interrupting the line at each quilted balloon.

Quilting Placement

4 Sew the binding strips end to end to make a continuous binding. Bind the edges of the quilt.

5 To display the wall quilt, sew a sleeve to the backing.

On the Lighter Side

To prevent show-through from the dark balloons and sashes under the light-colored balloons, use a lightweight fusible interfacing to line the light patches before appliquéing. Trace the patch on the fusible side of the interfacing, and cut on the marked line. Press the interfacing on the wrong side of the fabric. Use the interfacing as a guide to add ³⁄₁₆″ turn-under allowance all around, and cut out the patch. Press the allowance over the interfacing, and if you wish, baste in place.

Let It Snow!

This version is perfect for a holiday wall decoration. Fuse the appliqué patches for a quick project. Substitute white fabric for the brown to make a polar bear, add an appliquéd nose, and let him catch snowflakes.

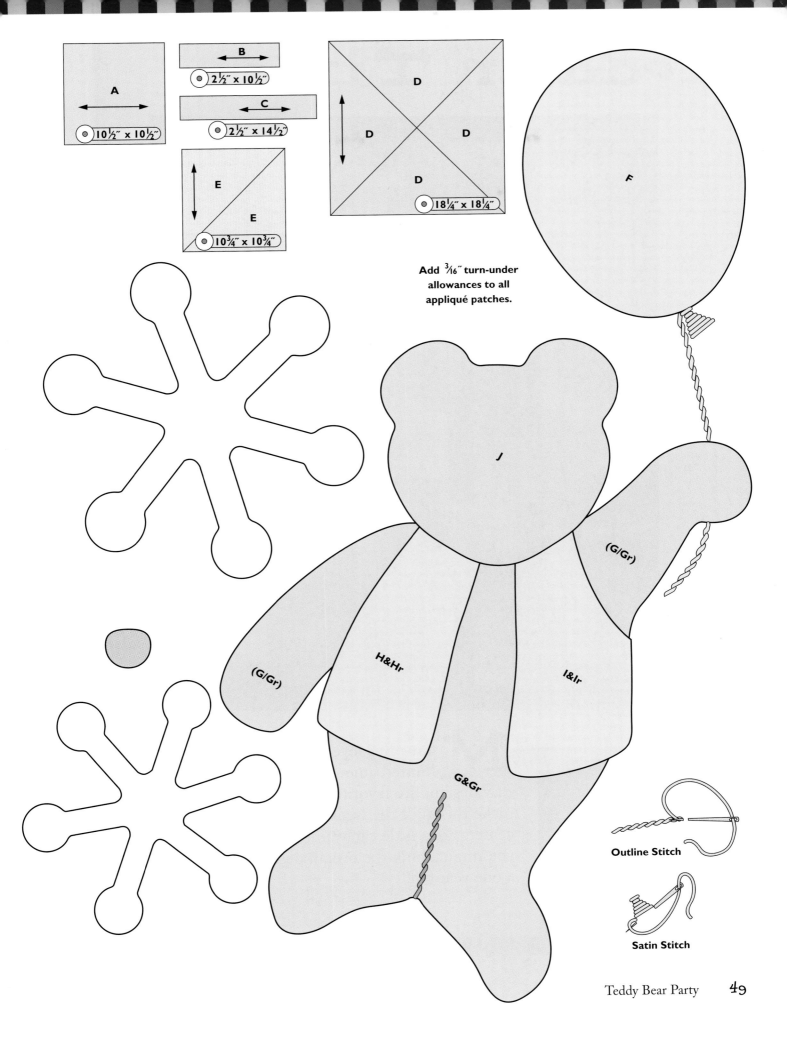

A

⊙ 10½″ x 10½″

B

⊙ 2½″ x 10½″

C

⊙ 2½″ x 14½″

E

E

⊙ 10¾″ x 10¾″

D

D   D

D

⊙ 18¼″ x 18¼″

Add ³⁄₁₆″ turn-under allowances to all appliqué patches.

F

J

(G/Gr)

(G/Gr)

H&Hr

I&Ir

G&Gr

Outline Stitch

Satin Stitch

Toddler Time

Many of us love making quilts for gifts but have a limited amount of sewing time, so quick-and-easy designs are favorites. With just four fabrics, you can make this quilt the week of the baby shower! The block centers are a little catawampus when arranged in rows—you might think the overall design looks like the walk of a one year old.

Designed by Caroline Reardon, made by Jonna Castle. Fabrics from Hoffman California Fabrics.

Materials and Cutting

QUILT SIZES:	Crib/Wall Quilt (shown)	Long Twin Comforter
	40½" × 48"	70½" × 93"
FINISHED BLOCK SIZE:		
7½" × 7½"		
YARDAGE		
Multiprint	⅔ yard	2 yards
	30 A	108 A
Pink Print	⅔ yard	2⅛ yards
	30 B, 30 D	108 B, 108 D
Blue Print	1 yard	3 yards
	30 C, 30 E	108 C, 108 E
Teal Print	1½ yards	2¾ yards
border sides*	2 at 2" × 47½"	2 at 2" × 92½"
border top/bottom*	2 at 2" × 43"	2 at 2" × 73"
double-fold binding	5 at 2¼" × 41"	4 at 2¼" × 88"
Backing	2¾ yards	5¾ yards
panels	2 at 27" × 45"	2 at 38" × 97"
sleeve	1 at 9" × 40"	none for this size
Batting	45" × 52"	75" × 97"

*An extra 2" have been added to the length for insurance.

Getting Started

For more detailed directions on quiltmaking, see Quilting Basics (pages 76–79).

Directions are for both the crib/wall quilt and the long twin comforter. Information specific to the twin size is given in brackets [ ].

This quilt is a perfect project for a baby quilt or child's room. Select cheery pastels with good contrast to show off the zigzag pattern.

Making the Top

1 Follow the Block Piecing diagram to make 30 [108] blocks. Press seam allowances away from the center. Join the blocks into 6 [12] rows, orienting them as shown in the Row diagram. Press seam allowances as shown. Turn every other row upside down, and join the rows. Press seam allowances all one way.

Block Piecing
Make 30 [108]

Row
Make 6 [12]
Crib quilt is shown in darker colors.
Long twin comforter includes the complete diagram.

2 Add the side border strips to the quilt, press seam allowances toward the strips, and trim the extra length. Add the top and bottom border strips, and press and trim as before.

Quilting and Finishing

1 Mark a Toddler Charm Tack in each A center.

2 Layer the backing, batting, and quilt top. Baste the layers together.

3 Quilt in-the-ditch the A's, the blocks, and the border; then quilt the marked motifs. To make the Charm Tacks stand out, use 2 matching strands of thread in your machine. If your machine has only 1 spindle, place the second spool in a cup at the back of your machine; then thread as usual.

4 Sew the binding strips end to end to make a continuous binding. Bind the edges of the quilt.

5 To display the wall quilt, sew a sleeve to the backing.

Scrap Medley

This scrap quilt approach could easily use a wide assortment of leftovers. To emphasize the graphic design of this pattern, first separate fabric candidates into lights, mediums, and darks; if any are questionable, do not use them.

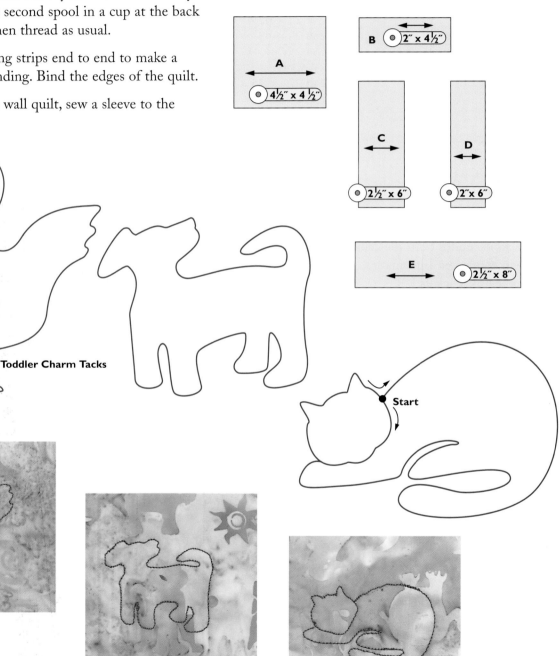

A — 4½" x 4½"

B — 2" x 4½"

C — 2½" x 6"

D — 2" x 6"

E — 2½" x 8"

Toddler Charm Tacks

Start

Barnyard

Designed by Becky Anderson, made by Maria Capp. Fabrics from Blank Textiles, Inc., and Robert Kaufman.

A little friend of Becky Anderson from Bloomington, Minnesota, asked Becky to make a quilt just for him. He had lots of little stuffed animal toys, so a quilt of barns with open doors was perfect. Each barn has a pocket where he can place his toys.

Materials and Cutting

QUILT SIZE:	Wall Quilt
	60" × 54"

FINISHED BLOCK SIZES:
3" × 12", 12" × 12"

YARDAGE

Assorted Scraps	
for each X block	1 A, 1 B
for each Y block	1 A, 1 C, 1 D, 1 E
for each Z block	4 H, 3 I
for the cat's head	2 at 2¾" × 3"
for the cat's body	2 at 4" × 4¾"
for the cow's head	2 at 2¾" × 3¼"
for the cow's body	2 at 4¼" × 5½"
for the lamb's head	2 at 2¾" × 2¾"
for the lamb's body	2 at 3¾" × 4"
for the pig's head	2 at 2¾" × 3¼"
for the pig's body	2 at 3½" × 4"
Muslin	⅞ yard
	9 E
Blue Print	1⅜ yards
	6 A, 18 F, 9 G, 12 H, 9 J, 9 Jr, 6 K
Medium Green Print	1⅞ yards
outer border sides*	2 at 3½" × 50½"
outer border top/bottom*	2 at 3½" × 62½"
sashes*	3 at 3½" × 53½"
Dark Green Print	1¾ yards
inner border sides*	2 at 2" × 47½"
inner border top/bottom*	2 at 2" × 56½"
double-fold binding	5 at 2¼" × 50"
Backing	3¾ yards
panels	2 at 30" × 64"
sleeve	1 at 9" × 60"
Batting	
for the quilt top	58" × 64"
for the Y blocks	22" × 40"

SUPPLIES: ¾" sew-through button for the pig's snout; embroidery floss, puff paint, or fabric pens for the other facial features; fiberfill stuffing

*An extra 2" have been added to the length for insurance.

Getting Started

For more detailed directions on quiltmaking, including the Y-seams in the barn blocks, see Quilting Basics (pages 76–79).

Choosing Fabrics and Making Blocks X and Z

1 Each silo (block X) in the photographed quilt is made from 2 of the fabrics used in the adjoining barn. To make a silo block, turn under the curved edge of a B patch ³⁄₁₆" and baste.

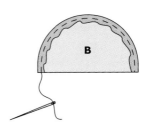

2 Center the B wrong side down on the right side of a blue A patch, aligning the raw edges. Sew a scrap A patch to the blue A, sandwiching the B patch in the middle. Press the seam allowances toward the scrap A. Appliqué the curved edge of B onto the blue A. Repeat to make 6 silo blocks.

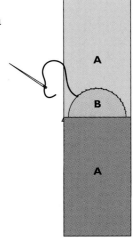

Block X
Make 6

3 To make the windmills (block Z) resemble the weathered ones found in ranchers' fields, we chose a dark gray scrap for each set of blades and a medium gray scrap for each windmill base. For added realism, the blades are three-dimensional. To make the blades for a windmill block, fold a scrap H patch, right side facing out, and baste in place on the right side of a blue H.

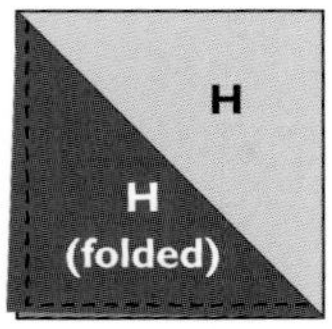

4 Repeat Step 3 to make 3 more blades. Sew these together to make the top of the windmill. Join the I, J, and Jr patches to make the base. Join the blades and base to complete your first windmill block. Make 2 more blocks like this.

Making the Y Blocks

1 Sew an A and a C patch together, stopping and backstitching ¼″ from the edge where the D patch will be set in. Add the D patch, sewing in the directions shown.

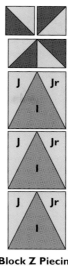

Block Z Piecing
Make 3

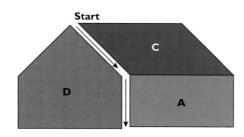

2 To make the barn into a pocket for toys, trace the door template on the wrong side of the D patch. Layer in this order: a batting E patch, a muslin E, and the barn centered right side down on the muslin.

3 Sew along the traced outline of the door. To make the opening for the door, cut out the doorway, leaving a ¼″ seam allowance. Trim the batting close to the stitches and clip the curve.

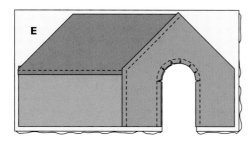

4 Turn the barn assembly right side out. Edge stitch around the door. Baste the layers together, close to the raw edges. Place the barn right side up on the right side of a scrap E patch. Join these pieces, sewing over the basting stitches. Trim the excess batting and the E patch fabrics even with the edges of the barn.

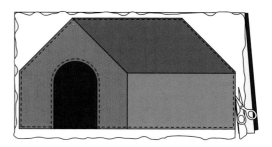

5 Sew 2 F patches to the barn. To complete the block, add a G patch.

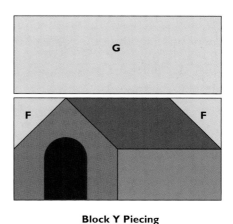

Block Y Piecing
Make 9

6 Make 8 more barn blocks this way.

Assembling the Quilt Top

1 Refer to the quilt in the photograph to join the K patches and blocks to make the rows. Match the centers and join the rows and sashes. Trim the excess length from the sashes.

2 For squared borders, match the centers, and sew an inner side border strip to a side of the quilt. Trim the excess fabric. Repeat for the other inner side border strip. Press the seam allowances toward the border strips. Add the top and bottom inner border strips. Trim and press. Sew the outer border strips to the quilt in the same order.

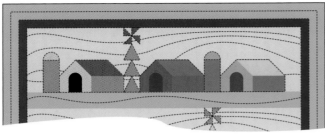

Quilting Placement

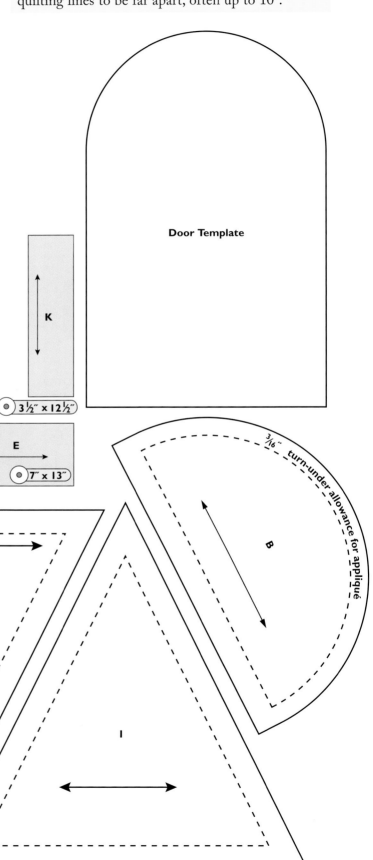

Quilting Tip

Needle-punched batting is sturdy and will hold up well in a play quilt. This type of batting allows quilting lines to be far apart, often up to 10″.

Quilting and Finishing

1 Layer the backing, batting, and quilt top. Baste the layers together.

2 Quilt in-the-ditch the silos, the outer edges of the barns, the windmill bases, and the inner border as shown. Quilt around the folded windmill blades. Quilt gentle curves in the sky and grass. Quilt the outer border 1½″ from the seamline.

3 Sew the binding strips end to end to make a continuous binding. Bind the edges of the quilt.

4 To display the quilt on a wall, sew a sleeve to the backing.

Door Template

K
○ 3½″ x 12½″

A
○ 3½″ x 6½″

3½″   C   3½″
3½″
○ 3½″ x 10¼″
3½″

Align arrows with lengthwise or crosswise grain of fabric.

E
○ 7″ x 13″

3¼″   3¼″
3¼″   3¼″
D   6⅝″
○ 6½″ x 6⅝″
— 6½″ —

J&Jr

I

3/16″ turn-under allowance for appliqué

B

F
F
○ 3⅞″ x 3⅞″

H
○ 2″ x 2″

G
○ 6½″ x 12½″

Sewing the Animals

The patches for these small stuffed animals are sewn first and then cut out.

1 Start with the cat and trace both her head and body separately onto tracing paper. Tape the paper to a sunny window or other light source. Place a 2¾" × 3" scrap wrong side up on the tracing and transfer the outline of the head onto the fabric. Turn over the fabric, align the traced outlines, and then transfer the eyes and nose.

2 Add the face details with embroidery, puff paint, or fabric pens. For embroidery, use 3 strands of floss to satin stitch the eyes and nose. If you use puff paint, let it dry as instructed by the manufacturer before continuing.

Satin Stitch   **Outline Stitch**

3 Place the 2 scraps for the cat's head right sides together. With a short stitch, sew along the line. To reinforce the stitching, sew over the line again. Trim the seam allowance to ⅛". Clip each inside point.

4 Make a slit approximately ¾" long on the wrong side of the head in an area that will be covered by the cat's body. Turn the head right side out through the slit.

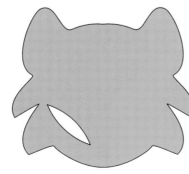

5 Make and turn the cat's body in the same way, cutting a slit approximately ¾" long in an area that will be covered by the cat's head.

Turning Tip

A mechanical pencil, with the lead retracted, or a clay tool from the craft store work well for turning the patches and for stuffing.

Repeat Steps 1–4 for the cow, lamb, and pig. Securely sew the ¾" button in place for the pig's snout.

Stuffing

1 Start with the cat's body and use small amounts of stuffing to fill in the legs and tail. Then add larger amounts until firmly stuffed. Repeat for the cat's head. Use a whipstitch to close the 2 slits.

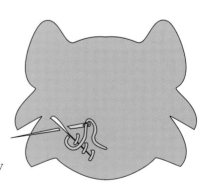

2 Stuff each animal in the same manner, beginning with small amounts of stuffing for the tiny areas like the ears, tails, and legs.

Completing the Animals

1 Tack each animal's head securely onto its body as shown, or tilt the head to one side to alter its expression.

Tuck Me In

Busy Baby

This eye-catching quilt will grab baby's attention when you use high-contrast fabrics. To make it a play-with-me quilt, create detachable toys for baby to explore. And for moms and babies on the go, a carrying handle allows the set to be packaged conveniently for traveling.

Designed and made by Vivian Ritter.
Modeled by Jessika Hoyberg-Nielsen.

Materials and Cutting

QUILT SIZE:	Crib Quilt
	32" × 32"
FINISHED BLOCK SIZE:	
9½" × 9½"	
YARDAGE	
Black, White, Red, and Yellow Prints	Assorted Scraps
hanging strips	7 at 1" × 6½"
blocks R–Z	1 A, 36 B**, 7 C, 4 D, 6 E,
	1 F, 1 G, 4 H**, 1 I, 3 J,
	4 K, 1 L, 1 M
Black-and-white Check	⅜ yard
border sides*	2 at 2¼" × 31"
border top/bottom*	2 at 2¼" × 34½"
Red-and-white Stripe	⅜ yard
double-fold binding	4 at 2¼" × 38"
Backing	1⅛ yards
panel	1 at 36" × 36"
Batting	36" × 36"

SUPPLIES: fusible web, polyester stuffing, ½ yard ¼"-wide grosgrain ribbon, 1" × 9" strip of hook-and-loop tape (such as Velcro); optional: plastic squeakers, electronic music box

*An extra 2" have been added to the length for insurance.
**You will need a 7" × 14" scrap for each set of 4 B's and a 4" × 8" scrap for the set of 4 H's.

Getting Started

For more detailed directions on quiltmaking, see Quilting Basics (pages 76–79).

To get the most contrast, which babies love, select fabrics and cut the patches for one block at a time. Cut the 4 B's in each block from the same fabric. Cut 4 H's that match for the V block.

Making the Blocks

1 Blocks S, U, and Y have strips for hanging the detachable toys. To make a hanging strip, fold under the raw edges on 3 sides as shown. Fold the strip lengthwise, with wrong sides together, and press. Topstitch to close. Sew the loop side of a 1" piece of hook-and-loop tape near the finished end of the strip. Sew the hook side about 1" from the other end. Make 2 more hanging strips.

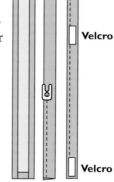

2 Directions for making each block center follow. For all blocks, sew B patches to opposite sides of each block center. Trim the corners as shown. Sew matching B's to the remaining sides.

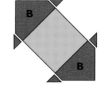

Block R: Sew strips to opposites sides of the A patch. Trim the excess length from the strips. Add strips to the remaining sides of A and press.

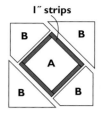

1" strips

Block R Piecing

Block S: Baste or fuse a D patch on a C patch. Stabilize by placing a sheet of typing paper underneath C. Satin stitch or zigzag stitch the D in place and remove the paper. Baste the raw edge of a hanging strip in place on an edge of C. Pin the length of the strip safely away from the seam allowances.

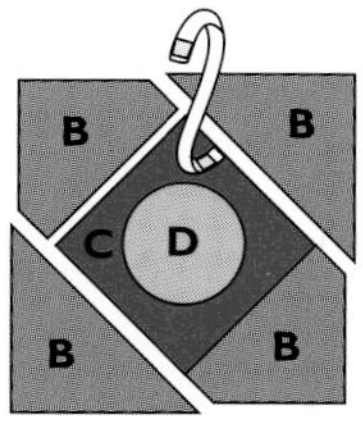

Block S Piecing

Block T: Join the E patches to make a Four-Patch.

Block U: Baste a hanging strip to the edge of the C patch and pin away from the seam allowances.

Block T Piecing

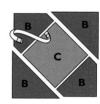

Block U Piecing

Block V: Matching corners, pin G right side up on F. Make a pleat on each side of G and pin and baste around the edges. (This is similar to the old "biscuit" patchwork.) Slit the F patch and insert the squeaker or some stuffing. Whipstitch the slit closed. Add the H patches as shown.

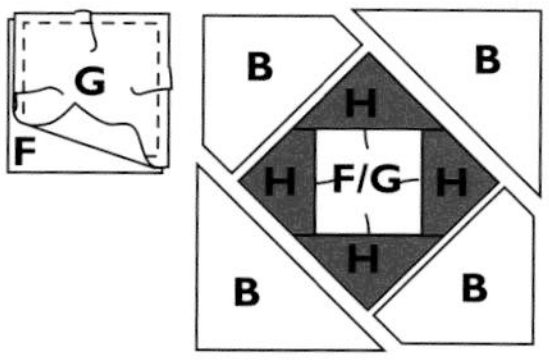

Block V Piecing

Block W: Add the I patch to a C patch in the same way you did for block S. Remove the paper.

Block X: Add the D patch to a C patch as you did for block S. Then add the J patch to D in the same way.

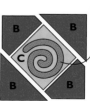

Block W Piecing

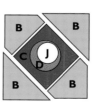

Block X Piecing

Block Y: Baste a hanging strip to the edge of a C patch. Pin the rest of the strip away from the seam allowances. Fold another C patch in half diagonally, wrong sides together. Align with the raw edges of the first C patch, covering the edge that has the hanging strip. Baste in place.

Block Y Piecing

Block Z: With right sides together, sew 2 E patches together on 3 sides. Turn right side out and fold in the raw edges. Enclose a squeaker. Topstitch this flap to a C patch along the open edge.

Block Z Piecing

*Two E patches sewn together, with squeaker inserted, then stitched to C

Making the Detachable Toys

1. The detachable toys are stuffed triangles and circles. Fold a 3″ piece of ribbon in half. Pin the ribbon in place on the right side of a K patch, matching raw edges. Stitch that K to another K (right sides together), leaving a side open for turning and catching the ribbon in the seam. Turn and fill with stuffing, a squeaker, or a music box. Whipstitch the opening closed. Use the remaining D, J, and K patches to make 3 more toys—a triangle, a large circle, and a small circle.

Whipstitch

2. You can use the fabric loops to attach rattles, teething rings, and other baby-safe toys.

Assembling the Quilt Top

1. Join 3 blocks to make each row. Make 3 rows, and join the rows as shown.

2. For squared borders, join the side border strips to both sides of the quilt. Trim the excess length and press the seam allowances toward the strips. Add the top and bottom border strips in the same way.

Quilting

1. The simple quilting motifs can be free-motion quilted without marking. If you prefer to mark, trace the lines in the B patches and in any other patches you wish.

2. Layer the backing, batting, and quilt top. Baste the layers together.

3. Quilt in-the-ditch the blocks and patches. Quilt the motifs as marked or freehand.

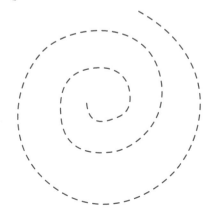 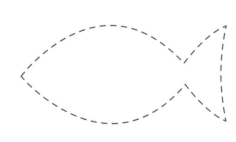 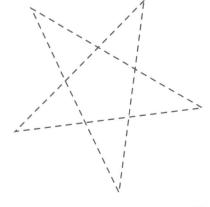

Adding the Handle

1 Fold L in half, right sides together. Sew along the 2 short ends. Turn right side out and press. Sew the hook side of a 6" length of hook-and-loop tape along the folded edge through all layers.

2 With right sides together, sew the M patch into a tube. Turn right side out, and turn in the raw edges at both ends.

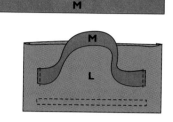

3 Topstitch along all 4 sides. Pin the handle ends on the side of L that does not have the hook-and-loop tape, about 1" from the edges as shown. Stitch the ends to L.

4 With the hook-and-loop tape facing up, center L/M on the top edge of the backing, aligning the raw edges. Baste in place. Stitch through all layers and sew the loop side of the 6" strip of hook-and-loop tape to the backing where shown. (Because the stitching is at the block seam, it will hardly show.)

Finishing Touches

1 Sew the binding strips end to end to make a continuous binding. Bind the edges of the quilt.

2 Hang toys from the loops in the blocks. Fold the quilt in thirds both ways, enclosing the toys. Fold the flap over to the backing, secure with the hook-and-loop tape, and you're ready to be on your way.

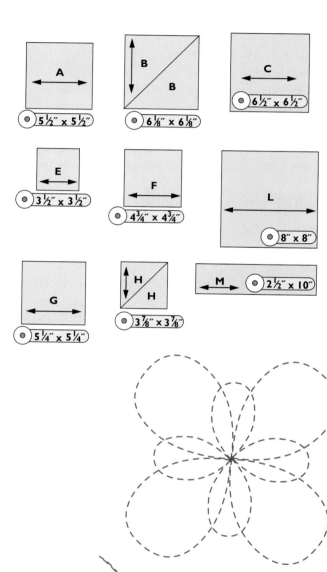

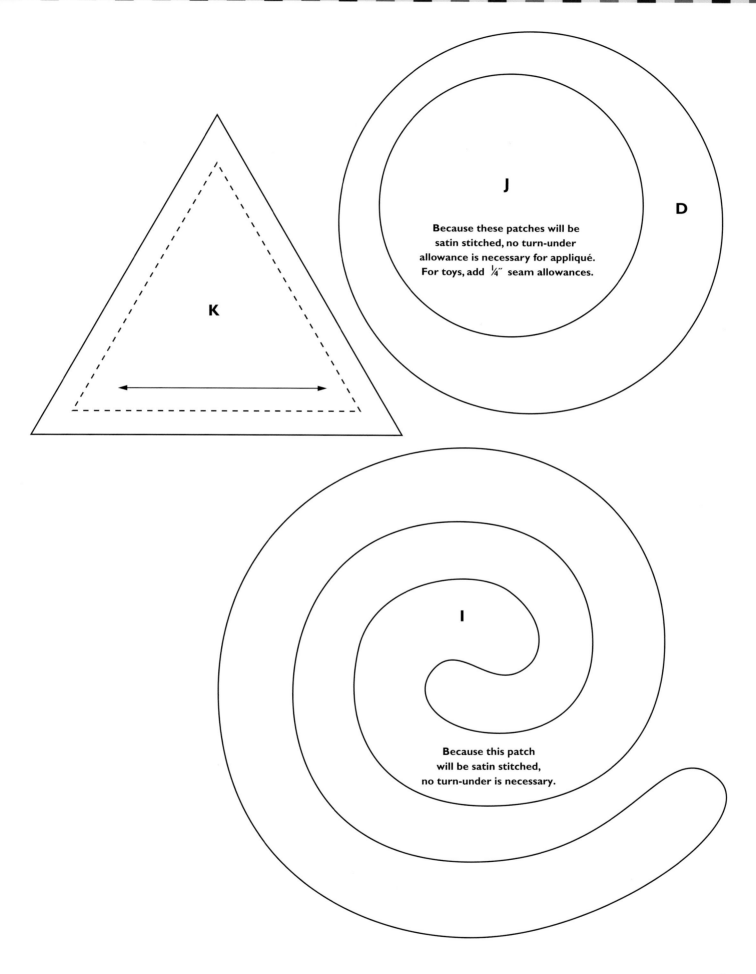

K

J

Because these patches will be satin stitched, no turn-under allowance is necessary for appliqué. For toys, add $\frac{1}{4}$″ seam allowances.

D

I

Because this patch will be satin stitched, no turn-under is necessary.

Penguin Party

Nancy Brown of Oakland, California, loves penguins and is always trying to find new ways to incorporate them into quilts. Most of her penguin designs are appliqué, so she wanted to try a pieced penguin for a change.

**Designed by
Nancy S. Brown,
sewn by Karen Alair.**

Materials and Cutting

	Crib/Wall Quilt (shown)	Twin Comforter
QUILT SIZES:	41" × 59"	69" × 96"
FINISHED BLOCK SIZE:		
9" × 9"		
YARDAGE		
Light Blue Print #1	⅝ yard	1½ yards
	6 A, 12 B, 12 C, 12 D, 6 E	22 A, 44 B, 44 C, 44 D, 22 E
Light Blue Print #2	⅝ yard	1¼ yards
	6 A, 12 B, 12 C, 12 D, 6 E	18 A, 36 B, 36 C, 36 D, 18 E
Medium Blue Print	¼ yard	¼ yard
	8 A, 16 B	8 A, 16 B
Dark Blue Print	1¾ yards	3⅛ yards
double-fold binding	4 at 2¼" × 56"	7 at 2¼" × 51"
outer border sides*	2 at 3½" × 55½"	2 at 5½" × 55½"
outer border top/bottom*	2 at 3½" × 43½"	2 at 5½" × 47½"
	15 A, 30 B	61 A, 132 B
White Print	½ yard	1 yard
	12 A, 12 D	40 A, 40 D
Yellow Print	½ yard	1 yard
	33 B	84 B
Gold Print	½ yard	1 yard
	33 B	84 B
Medium Orange Print	¼ yard	½ yard
	30 C	98 C
Dark Orange Print	1⅝ yards	1⅝ yards
inner border sides*	2 at 1½" × 53½"	2 at 1½" × 53½"
inner border top/bottom*	2 at 1½" × 37½"	2 at 1½" × 37½"
	30 C	102 C
Scrap Requirement for 1 Block:		
Dark Print Scrap**	4" × 10" scrap	4" × 10" scrap
	2 B, 2 C, 1 D	2 B, 2 C, 1 D
Backing	2⅔ yards	5⅞ yards
panels	2 at 32" × 45"	2 at 37" × 100"
sleeve	1 at 9" × 41"	none for this size
Batting	45" × 63"	73" × 100"

*An extra 2" have been added to the length for insurance.

**If you wish to use a single fabric rather than scraps for all penguins, you will need ¾ yard to cut 24 B, 24 C, and 12 D patches for the crib size. You will need 1¼ yards to cut 80 B, 80 C, and 40 D patches for the twin comforter.

Getting Started

For more detailed directions on quiltmaking, see Quilting Basics (pages 76–79).

All patches are specific in color except for the penguin heads and "coats." Have fun digging through your scrap collection to find a variety of prints in different colors to dress these penguins in tux and tails!

Constructing the Blocks and Units

1 Refer to the piecing diagrams for patch sewing sequence.

For the crib size, make 6 Y blocks, 6 Z blocks, 15 unit 1, 10 unit 2, and 8 unit 3.

OR

For the twin comforter, make 22 Y blocks, 18 Z blocks, 50 unit 1, 10 unit 2, 8 unit 3, 11 unit 4, 5 unit 5, and 5 unit 6.

Making Section 1

1 See the Section 1 Assembly diagram for the blocks and units needed and their orientation within the quilt.

2 Make 4 rows of penguins (Y and Z blocks) and 5 rows of unit 1's. Join these rows as shown.

3 Construct the pieced borders for the sides with unit 2's and 3's and join a side inner border strip to each. Trim excess border fabric. Sew these to the center portion. Add the top and bottom inner border strips. To complete section 1, add the sides and then the top and bottom outer border strips. The crib/wall quilt is now complete. Go to Step 1 of Quilting and Finishing. [For the twin size, go to Completing the Twin Comforter.]

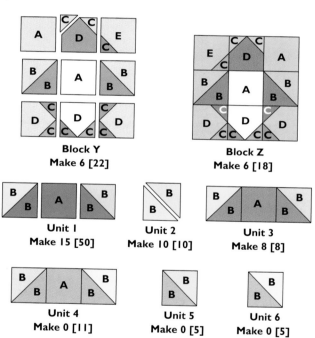

Block Y
Make 6 [22]

Block Z
Make 6 [18]

Unit 1
Make 15 [50]

Unit 2
Make 10 [10]

Unit 3
Make 8 [8]

Unit 4
Make 0 [11]

Unit 5
Make 0 [5]

Unit 6
Make 0 [5]

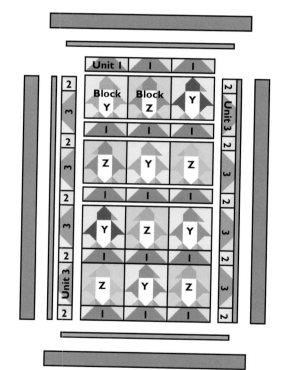

**Section 1
Crib/Wall Assembly**

Completing the Twin Comforter

1 Follow the assembly diagrams to make 2 section 2's, 1 section 3, and 1 section 4, orienting the units as shown.

Block Y	Block Z	Y	Z	Y	Z	Y
Unit 4	4	4	4	4	4	4

Section 2 Make 0 [2]

5	Unit 1	1	1	1	1	1	1	6
6	Unit 1	1	1	1	1	1	1	5
Unit 4	Block Y	Block Z	Y	Z	Y	Z	Y	Unit 4
5	Unit 1	1	1	1	1	1	1	6
6	Unit 1	1	1	1	1	1	1	5

Section 3 Make 0 [1]

Unit 4	Block Y	Block Z	Y	Z	Y	Z	Y	Unit 4
5	Unit 1	1	1	1	1	1	1	6

Section 4 Make 0 [1]

2 Refer to the Twin Comforter Assembly diagram and join the section 2's to the sides of section 1. Then add section 3 to the top of the quilt and section 4 to the bottom.

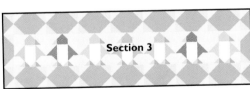

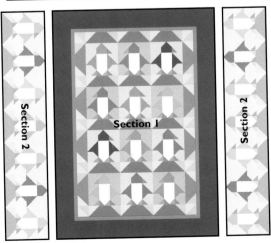

Section 3

Section 2

Section 1

Section 2

Section 4

Twin Comforter Assembly

Quilting and Finishing

1 Mark the *Catch of the Day* quilting motif at the center of each outer border strip. Work toward the corners to fit 9 motifs on each side at equal intervals and 7 motifs on the top and bottom strips.

2 Layer the backing, batting, and quilt top. Baste the layers together.

3 Quilt in-the-ditch the patches and border seamlines. Quilt in-the-ditch the patches and the motifs as marked.

Quilting Placement

4 Sew the binding strips end to end to make a continuous binding. Bind the edges of the quilt.

5 To display the wall-size quilt on a wall, sew a sleeve to the backing.

Speedy Triangles

The twin-size quilt includes lots of half-square triangles. To construct these, you might like to use a gridded 3"-finished half-square triangle paper, such as Triangles on a Roll. You'll spend less time piecing and get a high degree of accuracy!

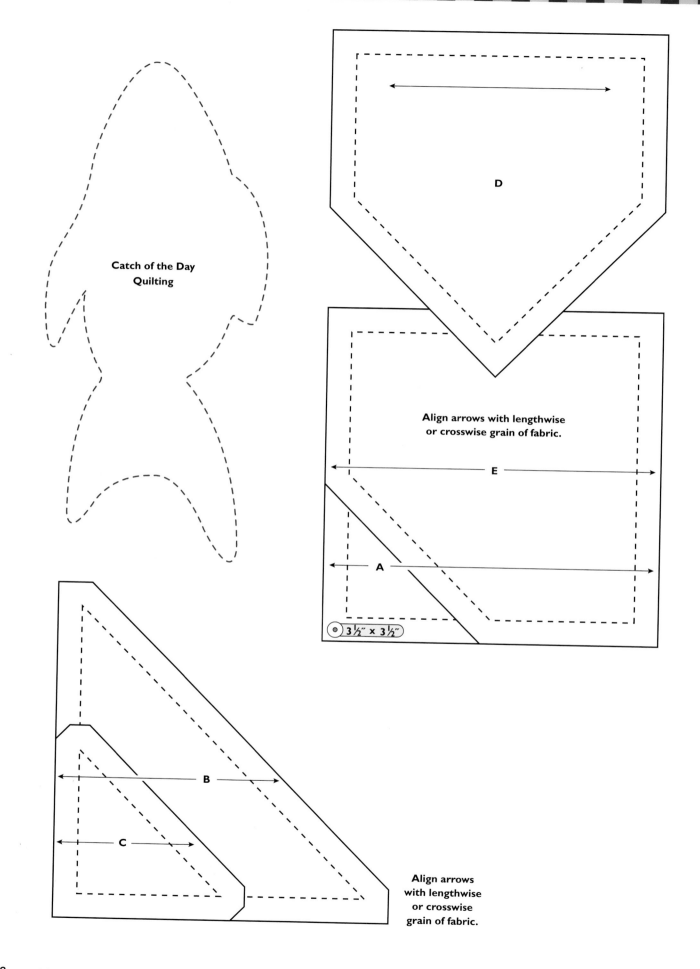

Catch of the Day
Quilting

D

Align arrows with lengthwise
or crosswise grain of fabric.

E

A

3½" x 3½"

B

C

Align arrows
with lengthwise
or crosswise
grain of fabric.

Winner's Circle

Designed and made by Caroline Reardon.

Winner's Circle is a perfect project for the equestrian in your life. Earthy, masculine colors like ours give it a great look for a man's den or a boy's room, or you can switch to pastels for that up-and-coming young horse lover. This update of a favorite pattern combines foundation piecing with traditional patchwork, making it as quick as a gallop around the corral!

QUILT SIZES:	Crib/Wall Quilt 44" × 44"	Long Twin Comforter (shown) 68" × 92"
FINISHED BLOCK SIZE:		
12" × 12"		
YARDAGE		
Dark Green Print	1⅛ yards	2⅝ yards
	20 A, 16 B, 16 Br, 20 C	68 A, 72 B, 72 Br, 68 C
Green and Beige Print**	⅞ yard	2⅛ yards
foundation piecing	background	background
Tan Multiprint	1 yard	2⅝ yards
	16 A, 20 B, 20 Br, 16 C	72 A, 68 B, 68 Br, 72C
Tan and Red Print**	⅞ yard	2⅛ yards
foundation piecing	background	background
Red Print	1½ yards	2¾ yards
border 2 sides*	2 at 2½" × 42½"	2 at 2½" × 90½"
border 2 top/bottom*	2 at 2½" × 46½"	2 at 2½" × 70½"
	4 C	4 C
Blue Print	½ yard	2⅝ yards
border 1 sides*	2 at 2½" × 38½"	2 at 2½" × 86½"
border 1 top/bottom*	2 at 2½" × 38½"	2 at 2½" × 62½"
Stripe	½ yard	¾ yard
double-fold binding	6 at 2¼" × 34"	9 at 2¼" × 40"
Prints	9 at ⅛ yard	35 at ⅛ yard
foundation piecing	horses	horses
Scraps	9 at 5" × 7"	35 at 5" × 7"
foundation piecing	manes and tails	manes and tails
Backing	3 yards	5¾ yards
panels	2 at 25" × 48"	2 at 37" × 96"
sleeve	1 at 9" × 44"	none for this size
Batting	48" × 48"	72" × 96"

*An extra 2" have been added to the length for insurance.
**For foundation piecing, extra yardage may be required.

Getting Started

For more detailed directions on quiltmaking, including foundation piecing, see Quilting Basics (pages 76–79).

Directions are for both the crib/wall quilt and the long twin comforter. Information that differs for the larger size is given in brackets [ ].

Use light and medium backgrounds for alternating blocks. When choosing prints for the horses, manes, and tails, make sure your fabrics contrast well with the backgrounds.

Making the Blocks and Rows

1 Make 9 [35] copies each of sections 1–4. You can either trace the pattern or use an accurate photocopy machine. Compare your copies with the original to ensure accuracy.

2 Follow the numerical order to machine piece the sections. Trim away the excess fabric and paper on the outer line of each foundation. Join the sections and press the seam allowances open. Sew the horses and patches together as shown to make the Y blocks and the Z blocks.

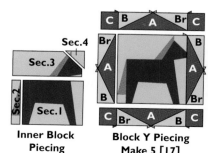

Inner Block Piecing

Block Y Piecing
Make 5 [17]

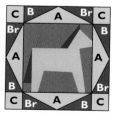

Block Z
Make 4 [18]

3 Refer to the diagrams for orientation, and join blocks to make the row 1's and row 2's. Press the seam allowances of every other row in the same direction. Sew the rows together, alternating types. Press these seam allowances in the same direction.

Row 1 Make 2 [4]

Row 2 Make 1 [3]

Top/Bottom Border 1 Make 2 [2]

Crib/wall quilt is shown in darker colors.
Long twin comforter includes the complete diagrams.

Adding the Borders

1 Lay the quilt flat and measure the width of the quilt from edge to edge through the center. Trim the top and bottom border 1 strips to this measurement and sew C patches to the ends of both strips. Press the seam allowances toward the strips.

2 Sew the border 1 side strips to the quilt. Press the seam allowances toward the strips and trim any extra length. Add the pieced top and bottom border 1 strips and press the allowances toward the strips. Add the border 2 strips—sides first and then the top and bottom strips. Trim and press as before. Carefully tear away the foundations.

Quilting and Finishing

1 Layer the backing, batting, and quilt top. Baste the layers together.

2 Quilt the horses in-the-ditch, and outline quilt the patches and borders as shown.

3 Sew the binding strips end to end to make a continuous binding. Bind the edges of the quilt.

4 To display the quilt on a wall, sew a sleeve to the backing.

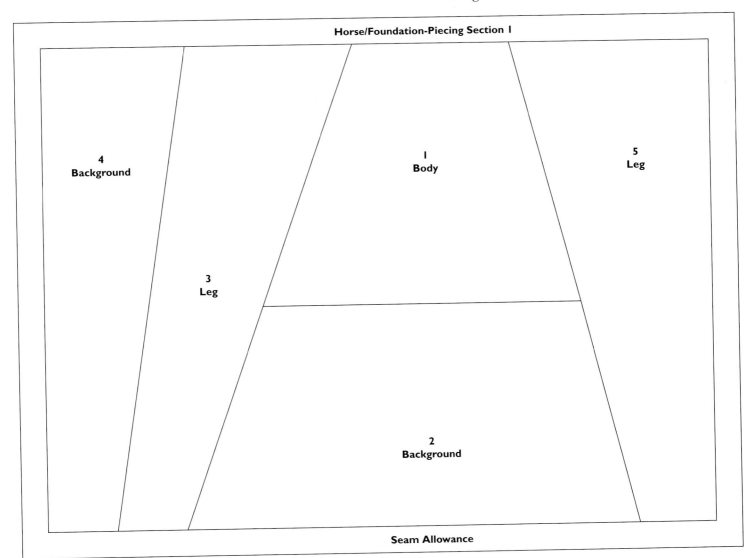

Horse/Foundation-Piecing Section 1

4 Background

3 Leg

1 Body

5 Leg

2 Background

Seam Allowance

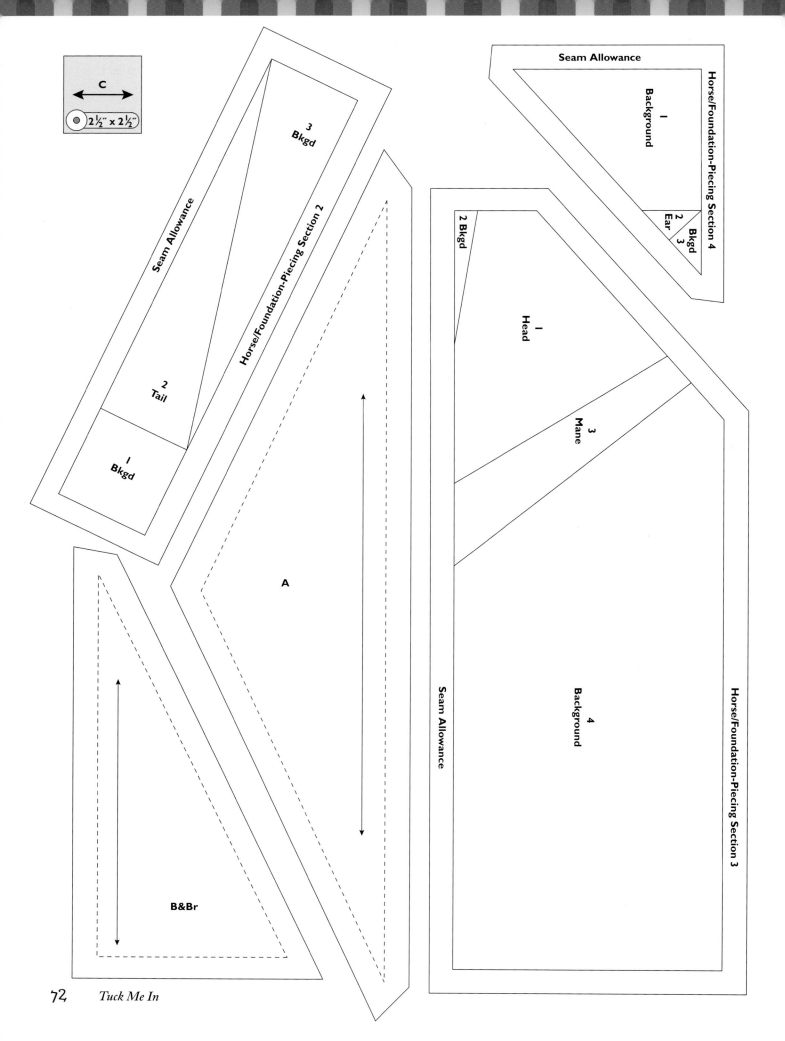

C

2½" x 2½"

3
Bkgd

Seam Allowance

Horse/Foundation-Piecing Section 2

2
Tail

I
Bkgd

A

B&Br

Seam Allowance

Horse/Foundation-Piecing Section 4

I
Background

2
Ear

Bkgd
3

2 Bkgd

I
Head

3
Mane

4
Background

Seam Allowance

Horse/Foundation-Piecing Section 3

Pass Kick Score

The oldest son of Elise Martin, from Indianapolis, Indiana, is an avid soccer player, so she wanted to reflect that in a quilt for his bed. She began the design by drawing the hexagons and pentagons in a soccer ball. Both Elise and her son are very satisfied with the results!

Designed by Elise Martin, sewn by Penny Wolf, and quilted by Shirley Wegert. Fabrics from South Sea Imports and Quilters Only, along with assorted scraps. Backing from Robert Kaufman.

CHALLENGING

QUILT SIZES:	Sofa Quilt (shown)	Twin Comforter
	54″ × 72″	63″ × 90″
FINISHED BLOCK SIZE:		
9″ × 9″		
YARDAGE		
White Print	2⅜ yards	3½ yards
inner border sides	2 at 1½″ × 65½″	2 at 1½″ × 83½″
inner border top/bottom	2 at 1½″ × 49½″	2 at 1½″ × 58½″
	35 B, 140 C	54 B, 216 C
Blue Prints for the border	2 yards	2½ yards
outer border sides*	2 at 4″ × 67½″	2 at 4″ × 85½″
outer border top/bottom*	2 at 4″ × 56½″	2 at 4″ × 65½″
Blue Prints for the blocks	12 at ⅛ yard**	18 at ⅛ yard**
from each fabric	9 A	9 A
Yellow Prints	12 at ⅛ yard**	18 at ⅛ yard**
from each fabric	9 A	9 A
Orange Print	⅝ yard	¾ yard
double-fold binding	8 at 2¼″ × 35″	9 at 2¼″ × 37″
Backing	3½ yards	5⅝ yards
panels	2 at 39″ × 58″	2 at 34″ × 94″
Batting	58″ × 76″	67″ × 94″

*An extra 2″ have been added to the length for insurance.
**If you wish to use fabrics you have on hand, 3 A patches require a 4½″ × 15″ scrap.

Getting Started

For more detailed directions on quiltmaking, see Quilting Basics (pages 76–79).

Directions are for both the sofa quilt and the twin comforter. Information that differs for the twin size is given in brackets [ ].

Making the Blocks

1 To make the blocks, first sort the A patches into sets of 3 of the same color. Use a set of both colors for each block, and make 35 [54] blocks.

First sew all A's to B. Stop at end of each seam-line and backstitch.

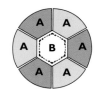

**Block Piecing
Make 35 [54]**

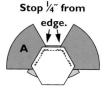 **Stop ¼″ from edge.**

 Sew in direction of arrow.

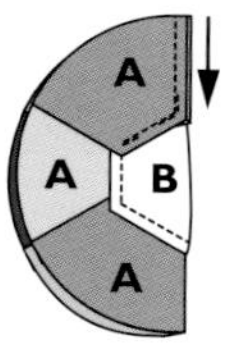

Join 4 C's and press allowances open. Then sew to A/B circle.

Assembling the Rows

1 For the sofa quilt, rotate the blocks as shown to make 4 row 1's and 3 row 2's. Beginning with a row 1 and alternating types, join the rows.

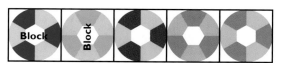

**Sofa Quilt Row 1
Make 4**

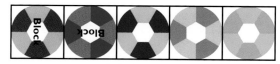

**Sofa Quilt Row 2
Make 3**

OR

For the twin comforter, make 9 rows. Turn every other row upside down and join the rows.

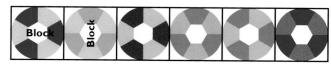

**Twin Comforter Row
Make 9**

Adding the Squared Borders

1 Sew the inner side border strips to the quilt, and trim the excess length. Press the seam allowances toward the border strips. Add the inner top and bottom border strips in the same way.

2 Join the outer border strips to the quilt as you did in Step 1.

Quilting and Finishing

1 Layer the backing, batting, and quilt top. Baste the layers together.

2 Quilt in-the-ditch the patches and the borders. Quilt a straight line in the outer border 1¾″ from the seamline.

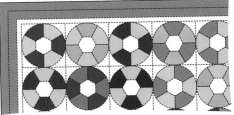

Quilting Placement

3 Sew the binding strips end to end to make a continuous binding. Bind the edges of the quilt.

Muted floral prints set the stage for a serene mood. In this design option, 3 of the patches in each circle are the same rose print in every block.

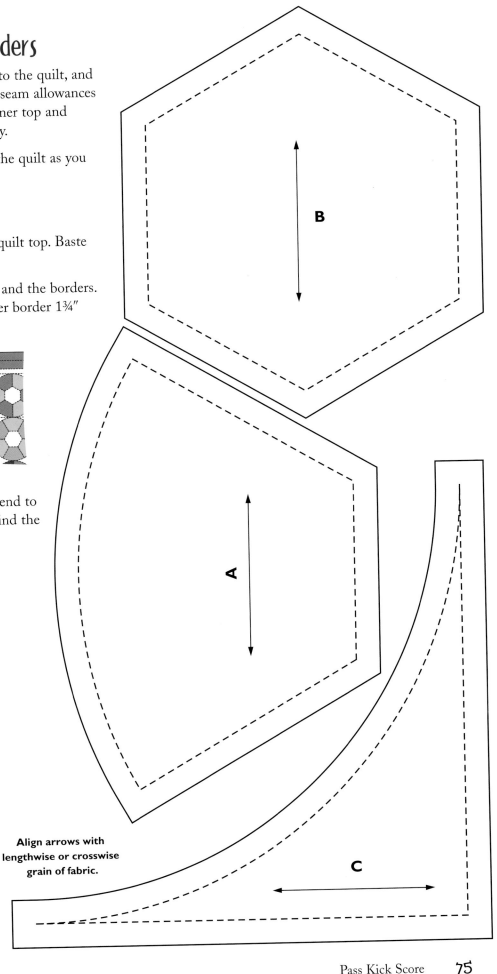

B

A

C

Align arrows with lengthwise or crosswise grain of fabric.

Quilting Basics

Fabric requirements are based on a 42″ width; note that many fabrics shrink when washed, and widths vary by manufacturer. In cutting instructions, strips are usually cut on the crosswise grain.

Seam Allowances

A ¼″ seam allowance is used for most projects. It's a good idea to do a test seam before you begin sewing to check that your ¼″ is accurate.

Pressing

In general, press seams toward the darker fabric. Press lightly in an up-and-down motion. Avoid using a very hot iron or ironing too much, which can distort shapes and blocks.

Y-Seams

Mark dots on the wrong side of the fabric ¼″ from the point of the triangle and from the corner of each diamond. These are the starting and stopping points of the Y-seams. Sew a diamond to the triangle unit. Backstitch at the dot. Press toward the diamond. Sew the other diamond to the opposite side of the triangle. Sew the two diamonds together, backstitching at the dot.

Mark dots on the triangle and diamonds.

Stitch to the dot and backstitch.

Press toward the diamond.

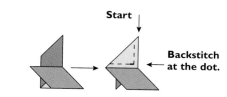

Sew the other diamond to the triangle.

Start

Backstitch at the dot.

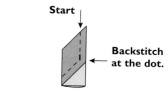

Start

Backstitch at the dot.

Sew the 2 diamonds together.

Press.

Borders

When border strips are to be cut on the crosswise grain, diagonally piece the strips together to achieve the needed lengths.

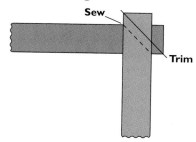

Sew

Trim

Diagonal Seam

Butted Borders

In most cases, sew on the side borders first. When you have finished the quilt top, measure it through the center vertically. This will be the length to cut the side borders. Place pins at the centers of all four sides of the quilt top, as well as in the center of each side border strip. Pin the side borders to the quilt top first, matching the center pins. Using a ¼″ seam allowance, sew the borders to the quilt top and press.

Measure horizontally across the center of the quilt top, including the side borders. This will be the length to cut the top and bottom borders. Repeat pinning, sewing, and pressing.

Backing

Plan on making the backing a minimum of 2″ larger than the quilt top on all sides. Prewash the fabric, and trim the selvages before you piece.

To economize, you can piece the back from any leftover fabrics or blocks in your collection.

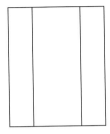

Twin

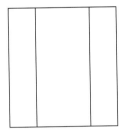

Full or Double

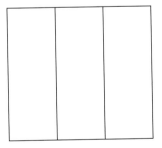

Queen or King

Batting

The type of batting to use is a personal decision; consult your local quilt shop. Cut batting approximately 2″ larger on all sides than your quilt top.

Layering

Spread the backing wrong side up, and tape down the edges with masking tape. (If you are working on carpet, you can use T-pins to secure the backing to the carpet.) Center the batting on top, smoothing out any folds. Place the quilt top right side up on top of the batting and backing, making sure it's centered.

Basting

If you plan to machine quilt, pin baste the quilt layers together with safety pins placed a minimum of 3″–4″ apart. Begin basting in the center, and move toward the edges in vertical, then horizontal, rows.

If you plan to hand quilt, baste the layers together with thread using a long needle and light-colored thread. Knot one end of the thread. Using stitches approximately the length of the needle, begin in the center and move out toward the edges.

Quilting

Quilting, whether by hand or machine, enhances the pieced or appliquéd design of the quilt. You may choose to quilt in-the-ditch, echo the pieced or appliqué motifs, use patterns from quilting design books and stencils, or do your own free-motion quilting. Suggested quilting patterns are included in some of the projects.

Binding

Double-Fold Straight-Grain Binding (French Fold)

1 Trim excess batting and backing from the quilt. If you want a ¼″ finished binding, cut the strips 2¼″ wide, and piece them together with a diagonal seam to make a continuous binding strip (see Borders on previous page).

2 Press the seams open, then press the entire strip in half lengthwise with wrong sides together. With raw edges even, pin the binding to the edge of the quilt a few inches from the corner, leaving the first few inches of the binding unattached. Start sewing, using a ¼″ seam allowance.

3 Stop ¼″ from the first corner, backstitch 1 stitch. Lift the presser foot and needle.

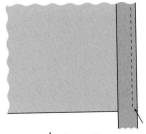

Stitch to ¼″ from the corner.

4 Rotate the quilt one-quarter turn. Fold the binding at a right angle so it extends straight above the quilt.

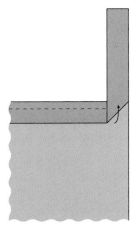

First fold for miter

5 Then bring the binding strip down even with the edge of the quilt (see Step 3). Repeat in the same manner at all corners. Begin sewing at the folded edge.

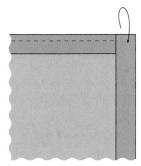

**Second fold alignment
Repeat in the same manner at all corners.**

Finishing the Binding

Method 1
Fold under the beginning end of the binding strip ¼". Lay the ending binding strip over the beginning folded end. Continue stitching beyond the folded edge. Trim the excess binding. Fold the binding over the raw edges to the quilt back and hand stitch, mitering the corners.

Method 2
1 Fold the ending tail of the binding back on itself where it meets the beginning binding tail. From the fold, measure and mark the cut width of your binding strip. Cut the ending binding tail to this measurement. For example, if your binding is cut 2¼" wide, measure from the fold on the ending tail of the binding 2¼", and cut the binding tail to this length.

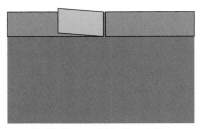

**Fold, then cut binding tail
to cut width of binding.**

2 Open both tails. Place one tail on top of the other tail at right angles, right sides together. Mark a diagonal line and stitch on the line. Trim the seam to ¼". Press open.

Stitch the binding ends diagonally.

Machine Appliqué Using Fusible Web

1 Place the fusible web sheet paper-side up on the pattern, and trace with a pencil. Trace detail lines with a permanent marker for ease in transferring to the fabric.

2 Use paper-cutting scissors to roughly cut out the pieces. Leave at least a ¼" border.

3 Follow the manufacturer's instructions to fuse the web patterns to the wrong side of the appliqué fabric. It helps to use an appliqué pressing sheet to avoid getting the adhesive on your iron or ironing board.

4 Cut out the pieces along the pencil line. Do not remove the paper yet.

5 Transfer the detail lines to the fabric by placing the piece on a light table or up to the window and marking the fabric. Use pencil for this task—the lines will be covered by thread.

6 Remove the paper backing and position the appliqué piece on your project. Be sure the web (rough) side is down. Press in place, following the manufacturer's instructions.

Paper Piecing

Once you get used to it, paper piecing is an easy way to ensure that your blocks are accurate. You sew on the side of the paper that has printed lines. You place the fabric on the nonprinted side.

1 Trace or photocopy the number of paper-piecing patterns needed for your project.

2 Use a smaller-than-usual stitch length (1.5–1.8, or 18–20 stitches per inch) and a slightly larger needle (size 90/14). This makes the paper removal easier and will result in tighter stitches that can't be pulled apart when you tear off the paper.

3 Cut the fabric pieces slightly larger than necessary—about ¾" larger; they do not need to be perfect shapes (one of the joys of paper piecing!).

With paper piecing, you don't have to worry about the grain of the fabric. You are stitching on paper and that stabilizes the block. The paper is not torn off until after the blocks are stitched together.

4 Follow the number sequence when piecing. Pin the first piece in place on the blank side of the paper, but make sure you don't place the pin anywhere near a seamline. Hold the paper up to the light to make sure the piece covers the area it is supposed to, with the seam allowance also amply covered.

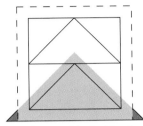
Pin first piece on blank side of paper.

5 Fold the pattern back at the stitching line, and use a ruler and rotary cutter to trim the fabric to a ¼" seam allowance.

6 Cut the second piece large enough to cover the area plus a generous seam allowance. It's a good idea to cut each piece larger than you think necessary; it might be a bit wasteful, but it's easier than ripping out tiny stitches!

Align the edge with the trimmed seam allowance of the first piece, right sides together, and pin. With paper side up, stitch 1 line.

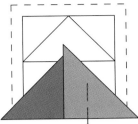
Place and pin second piece.

7 Open the second piece and press.

8 Continue stitching each piece in order, being sure to fold back the paper pattern and trim the seam allowance to ¼" before adding the next piece.

9 Trim all around the finished unit to the ¼" seam allowance. Leave the paper intact until after you have sewn the blocks together, then carefully remove it. Creasing the paper at the seamline helps when tearing it.

Paper-Piecing Hints

- When making several identical blocks, it helps to work in assembly line fashion. Add the first and second pieces to each of the blocks, then add the third piece and so on.
- Precutting all the pieces at once is a time saver. Make one block first to ensure that each fabric piece will cover the area needed.
- When piecing a dark and a light fabric together where the seam allowance needs to be pressed toward the light fabric, the edge of the dark seam allowance will sometimes show through the light fabric. To prevent this, trim the dark seam allowance about ¹⁄₁₆" narrower than the light seam allowance.

Resources

Organizations That Provide Quilts for Children in Need

ABC Quilts
phone: 800-536-5694
email: info@abcquilts.org
website: www.abcquilts.org

Binky Patrol
website: www.binkypatrol.com

Project Linus
phone: 309-664-7814
email: information@
　　　projectlinus.org
website: www.projectlinus.org

Quilts for Kids, Inc
phone: 215-295-5484
email: quiltsforkids@snip.net
website: www.quiltsforkids.org

Quilting Supplies

Cotton Patch Mail Order
3405 Hall Lane, Dept. CTB
Lafayette, CA 94595
phone: 800-835-4418;
　　　925-283-7883
email: quiltusa@yahoo.com
website: www.quiltusa.com

Note: Fabrics used in the quilts shown may not be currently available since fabric manufacturers keep most fabrics in print for only a short time.

For more information, write for a free catalog:

C&T Publishing, Inc.
P.O. Box 1456
Lafayette, CA 94549
phone: 800-284-1114
email: ctinfo@ctpub.com
website: www.ctpub.com

About the Author

Quiltmaker magazine has been providing quilters with patterns for a wide variety of quilts since 1982. Founded by Bonnie Leman as a sister magazine to *Quilter's Newsletter Magazine*, it offers creative designs for quilters of all levels, in sizes from crib to king.

Quiltmaker is known for step-by-step instructions that include quick and easy techniques, full-size templates, and rotary-cutting diagrams. Under the direction of current editor Brenda Bauermeister Groelz, *Quiltmaker* continues to please its readers with fresh patterns in up-to-date fabrics.

Quiltmaker magazine is a publication of the Primedia Enthusiast Group. For more about *Quiltmaker*, visit their website www.quiltmaker.com.

Other fine books by C&T Publishing and Primedia Enthusiast Group:

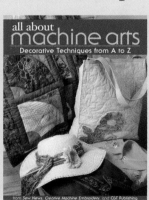